Gardening
Month by Month
in the
Maritimes

Duncan Kelbaugh
Alison Beck

Lone Pine Publishing

© 2004 by Lone Pine Publishing
First printed in 2004 10 9 8 7 6 5 4 3 2 1
Printed in Canada

All rights reserved. No part of this work covered by the copyrights hereon may be reproduced or used in any form or by any means—graphic, electronic or mechanical—without the prior written permission of the publishers, except for reviewers, who may quote brief passages. Any request for photocopying, recording, taping or storage on information retrieval systems of any part of this work shall be directed in writing to the publisher.

The Publisher: Lone Pine Publishing

10145 – 81 Avenue   1808 B Street NW, Suite 140
Edmonton, AB T6E 1W9 Canada   Auburn, WA, USA 98001
Website: www.lonepinepublishing.com

National Library of Canada Cataloguing in Publication

Kelbaugh, Duncan, 1953-
 Gardening month by month in the Maritimes / Duncan Kelbaugh, Alison Beck.
 ISBN 1-55105-408-6

1. Gardening—Maritime Provines—Calendars. 2. Gardening—Maritime Provinces.
 I. Beck, Alison, 1971- II. Title.
SB453.3.C2K44 2004   635'.09715   C2003-907172-3

Editorial Director: Nancy Foulds
Project Editor: Sandra Bit
Researchers: Don Williamson, Laura Peters
Production Manager: Gene Longson
Book Design & Layout: Heather Markham
Maps & Climate Charts: Elliot Engley,
 Chia-Jung Chang

Cover Design: Gerry Dotto
Principal Photographers: Tamara Eder,
 Tim Matheson
Illustrations: Ian Sheldon
Scanning & Digital Film: Elite Lithographers Co.

Front cover photographs (clockwise from top right): by Tamara Eder, 'Morden Sunrise'; *by Tim Matheson* coreopsis; *by Tamara Eder,* poppy, blanket flower, *Heliopsis,* sunflower, poppy; *by Tim Matheson,* daylily

The photographs in this book are reproduced with the generous permission of their copyright holders

All other photos: All-American Selections 99c, 129a; Sandra Bit 81a; Therese D'Monte 70; Don Doucette 15b, 23b, 39c, 147b; Elliot Engley 31b&d, 33a&b; EuroAmerican 19a; Jennifer Fafard 123c, 125b&c, 127a, 129c, 131c, 132–33, 151b, 155c; Derek Fell 4–5, 5a, 35b, 75b, 137b; Anne Gordon 137c; Chris Graham 39b; Saxon Holt 31a, 148; Duncan Kelbaugh 6–7, 7b&c, 35a, 51b, 57b, 75a, 83b, 101c, 117a, 147a; Linda Kershaw 36–37; Colin Laroque 96–97; Dawn Loewen 117b; Heather Markham 21a; Marilynn McAra 3, 51c, 115a&d; Steve Nikkila 131a; ©2004 Nova-Photo Graphik/Horticolor 94; Kim Patrick O'Leary 29b, 87b, 149a; Alison Penko 27a, 60–61, 113c, 139c 143; Laura Peters 79a, 119c, 147c, 149d, 151a&c, 153b, 155a&b; Robert Ritchie 59a, 137a; Pete Thompstone 45b, 111a; Don Williamson 119a, 135b.

Frost date and hardiness zone maps: information taken from *The Atlas of Canada* (http://atlas.gc.ca ©2002 . Her Majesty the Queen in Right of Canada with permission of Natural Resources Canada *Climate normals and extremes charts:* adapted from the Meteorological Service of Canada, with permission from Environment Canada (http://www.climate.weatheroffice.ec.gc.ca/climate_normals index_e.html).

This book is not intended as a 'how-to' guide for eating garden plants. No plant or plant extract should be consumed unless you are certain of its identity and toxicity and of your potential for allergic reactions.

We acknowledge the financial support of the Government of Canada through the Book Publishing Industry Development Program (BPIDP) for our publishing activities.

PC: 01

INTRODUCTION

Growing up, I spent most of each summer on my uncle's dairy farm in Quispamsis, N.B. I remember pulling up new carrots in the great big vegetable garden, wiping them 'clean' on my shirt, and tasting their delicious baby carrot flavour. I've been digging in the dirt ever since; my hands only come clean in January, when winter forces us inside. But that's what I really like about gardening here—that chance to relax, reflect on the successes and failures of last season, and plan a new and better attack for next year. No wonder we're so anxious to get outdoors and back into the mud come spring!

Maritime gardeners enthusiastically take advantage of the many assets the region offers while overcoming the challenges. Salt-laden air and sea spray, cooling fog, thin soil, short growing seasons, and storms from the north and south are challenges met and overcome by Maritime gardeners.

The Maritime provinces offer a diverse landscape, from the rich red soils of P.E.I. to the rocky coastlines of New Brunswick and Nova Scotia. Mixed forests of fir, spruce, birch, maple, pine and oak still occupy the land in much of this region even after centuries of settlement. Though the ground is often rocky, the arable valleys and acidic soil found in all three provinces support many of our favourite trees, shrubs and perennials.

One of the first steps in knowing what will grow well in your garden is knowing what grows naturally. Native plants and those that naturalize, occurring in places like wilderness areas or vacant lots, give you an indication of what will thrive in your garden. Look also at other gardens. The variety of plant material and designs displayed in Maritime gardens is a testimony to the broad selection gardeners here have to choose from.

Every imaginable style of garden can be and probably has been created here. Free-form English-style cottage gardens, formal knot gardens, woodland gardens and Zen-like Japanese

tulips

gardens all reflect the style and enthusiasm of the gardeners who create them and the diversity of situations in which they garden.

Where we garden varies almost as much as what we garden. Apartment and condo dwellers enjoy container gardening; rural gardeners may be tilling the same soil that many generations of their ancestors did; urban gardens include those older neighbourhoods with deeper topsoil and those whose brand new gardens may have only the thin layer of soil the construction company returned to their yards. Beautiful, successful gardens are possible in every situation, limited only by the imagination of the gardener.

The Canadian hardiness zone map places the Maritime provinces in zones 2, 3, 4, 5 and 6. Possible winter lows range from −39° to −18° C. While it's useful to know this when selecting plants for your garden, this designation is just a starting point for determining the hardiness of any given plant. Precipitation, soil conditions and

Shirley poppies

microclimates in your yard have an equal influence.

The Maritime climate is indeed excellent for growing many plants, but can still be challenging. Some research and experimentation are required to get the best results from your garden. Lack of consistent snowcover in some areas, cycles of freezing and thawing in winter and violent storms bringing rain or snow are all climatic challenges Maritime gardeners face. Learning what to expect and when to expect it as well as what plants are best suited to your garden are key elements to success.

gazanias

seaside garden (*above*); mini alpine garden (*below*)

naturalistic water feature (*below*)

During the growing season, adequate precipitation can make the difference between gardening success or failure. Most years regular rainfall takes care of all our watering needs and only hanging baskets and plants beneath the overhang of the house need to be watered. In a bad year, it seems as if it will never stop raining or that it will never rain again. Although rainfall is usually dependable, dry spells in mid and late summer and deluges in spring and fall do occur. As with all the factors that influence our gardens, we must be prepared to make the most of what nature offers us and try to take up the slack where it lets off.

The last spring frost usually occurs in late May and the first fall frost by October 1. Our 'safe planting date' for frost-tender plants is May 24, though rare frost may occur after this date.

The growing season ranges from 130 days in a cold year to 200 days in a warm year.

Though soil type and climate can limit our plant selections, it is possible to find or create a special spot in your garden for plants that aren't hardy or that don't like your soil. Planning an entire garden around these more difficult plants results in a lot of extra work, but a small area set aside for just a few such plants is part of the adventure of gardening. Hedges block the wind, trees give shade and raised beds provide deep soil. Know your garden and what it supports, but avoid being limited by it.

The purpose of this book is to give you ideas and to help you plan what should be done and when. Garden tasks are listed in the month they should be completed, and general ideas that can be applied in a variety of months are also included. There is plenty of space for you to write in your own thoughts and ideas.

mixed border

The information in this book is general. If you need more detailed information on a topic, refer to the resources listed at the back of the book. Your local library is also an excellent place to search for the information you need. Gardening courses are offered through colleges, continuing education programs

golden marguerite

a secret garden

crocuses herald the coming of spring

hot peppers

ardening clubs and most garden cen-
es. You can tackle even the most
aunting garden task once you are
repared and well informed.

Whether you live in a downtown
partment, a small suburban bunga-
w or a large country house with
cres of land, you can garden.
eautiful gardens are possible in all
cations. This monthly guide should
nswer some of your specific questions
bout the wonderful gardening possi-
lities in the Maritimes. By adding
our own particular garden notes to
ese pages—such as unusual weather
onditions, when plants sprout and
rst flower and the birds and insects
ou see in your garden—you will cre-
e your own custom-made gardening
ide.

Above all else, enjoy your Maritime
rden!

MARITIMES CLIMATE NORMALS 1971–2000
(Adapted from the Meteorological Service of Canada data
as posted on the Environment Canada website)

	CATEGORY	JAN	FEB	MAR	APR	MAY	JUN	JUL	AUG	SEP	OCT	NOV	DEC	YEAR
BATHURST	DAILY MAXIMUM (°C)	-6.1	-4.3	1.3	6.8	15.4	21.4	24.7	23.4	17.8	11.2	4.0	-3.3	9.4
	DAILY MINIMUM (°C)	-16.1	-14.7	-8.7	-2.0	4.2	10.2	13.8	12.9	7.8	2.4	-2.9	-12.0	-0.4
	RAINFALL (MM)	23.5	10.2	30.0	57.3	78.5	83.5	99.0	101.6	71.7	89.0	65.0	35.3	744.4
	SNOWFALL (CM)	69.0	53.1	54.3	33.4	1.0	0.0	0.0	0.0	0.0	0.6	30.3	72.5	314.2
	*PRECIPITATION (MM)	92.5	63.3	84.3	90.7	79.5	83.5	99.0	101.6	71.7	89.5	95.3	107.8	1058.6
FREDERICTON	DAILY MAXIMUM (°C)	-4.0	-2.3	3.0	9.7	17.5	22.8	25.6	24.7	19.5	12.8	5.6	-1.1	11.2
	DAILY MINIMUM (°C)	-15.5	-14.1	-7.8	-1.1	4.7	9.6	13.0	12.1	6.7	1.2	-3.5	-11.4	-0.5
	RAINFALL (MM)	46.2	32.2	48.1	64.1	94.2	88.6	87.1	89.8	94.5	96.0	85.5	59.4	885.5
	SNOWFALL (CM)	70.2	50.6	54.4	22.5	1.5	0.0	0.0	0.0	0.0	1.5	18.5	57.3	276.5
	PRECIPITATION (MM)	109.6	79.2	102.7	87.4	95.9	88.6	87.1	89.8	94.5	97.7	103.2	107.8	1143.3
GRAND FALLS	DAILY MAXIMUM (°C)	-8.3	-5.9	0.1	7.1	16.2	20.9	23.3	22.2	16.6	9.7	2.2	-5.3	8.2
	DAILY MINIMUM (°C)	-17.7	-15.6	-9.5	-1.7	5.0	9.9	12.8	11.8	6.7	1.9	-4.3	-13.7	-1.2
	RAINFALL (MM)	22.8	10.7	34.4	52.6	85.4	101.2	117.5	126.8	99.6	89.5	61.0	32.8	834.3
	SNOWFALL (CM)	71.6	55.1	47.0	24.8	0.7	0.0	0.0	0.0	0.0	1.8	31.1	67.9	300.1
	PRECIPITATION (MM)	94.4	65.8	81.5	77.5	86.2	101.2	117.5	126.8	99.6	91.3	92.1	100.8	1134.4
MONCTON	DAILY MAXIMUM (°C)	-3.6	-2.7	2.0	8.0	15.9	21.3	24.5	23.8	18.8	12.4	5.6	-0.7	10.4
	DAILY MINIMUM (°C)	-14.3	-13.2	-7.8	-1.7	3.9	8.9	12.6	12.0	7.2	1.8	-2.9	-10.3	-0.3
	RAINFALL (MM)	41.5	26.8	45.9	57.2	91.5	91.5	103.3	79.5	92.7	99.5	81.1	54.9	865.4
	SNOWFALL (CM)	80.1	68.1	70.8	35.8	4.5	0.0	0.0	0.0	0.0	3.4	21.7	65.6	349.9
	PRECIPITATION (MM)	119.2	92.9	123.6	99.3	97.1	91.5	103.3	79.5	92.7	103.8	104.5	115.8	1223.2
SAINT JOHN	DAILY MAXIMUM (°C)	-2.7	-1.9	2.3	8.3	14.8	19.5	22.4	22.2	17.7	11.9	6.0	0.3	10.1
	DAILY MINIMUM (°C)	-13.6	-12.7	-7.3	-1.2	4.0	8.4	11.7	11.6	7.7	2.7	-2.1	-9.7	-0.1
	RAINFALL (MM)	78.2	48.8	71.7	81.7	115.9	100.9	101.5	89.6	117.4	122.6	121.6	98.2	1147.9
	SNOWFALL (CM)	66.5	50.0	47.4	22.2	1.4	0.0	0.0	0.0	0.0	2.2	12.5	54.7	256.9
	PRECIPITATION (MM)	139.4	94.0	117.9	104.2	117.5	100.9	101.5	89.6	117.4	124.8	133.7	149.4	1390.3
HALIFAX	DAILY MAXIMUM (°C)	-1.2	-1.1	3.0	8.4	15.0	20.3	23.6	23.3	18.8	12.7	6.9	1.4	11.0
	DAILY MINIMUM (°C)	-10.7	-10.2	-5.8	-0.5	4.5	9.6	13.5	13.5	9.3	3.8	-0.7	-7.1	1.6
	RAINFALL (MM)	100.6	69.0	96.4	96.1	106.2	98.3	102.2	92.7	103.6	126.4	133.0	114.5	1238.9
	SNOWFALL (CM)	54.6	50.1	41.1	20.9	3.3	0.0	0.0	0.0	0.0	2.3	14.4	43.9	230.5
	PRECIPITATION (MM)	149.2	114.4	134.5	118.3	109.7	98.3	102.2	92.7	103.6	128.7	146.0	154.8	1452.2

*equivalent to rainfall

MARITIMES CLIMATE NORMALS 1971–2000
(Adapted from the Meteorological Service of Canada data
as posted on the Environment Canada website)

KENTVILLE

CATEGORY	JAN	FEB	MAR	APR	MAY	JUN	JUL	AUG	SEP	OCT	NOV	DEC	YEAR
DAILY MAXIMUM (°C)	-1.2	-0.9	3.4	9.5	16.3	21.6	24.8	24.2	19.4	13.4	7.5	1.6	11.6
DAILY MINIMUM (°C)	-9.8	-9.5	-5.2	0.4	5.4	10.5	14.0	13.5	9.2	4.5	0.1	-6.5	2.2
RAINFALL (MM)	60.2	45.0	63.9	70.5	92.7	81.4	87.6	85.5	87.3	93.3	103.7	77.0	948.0
SNOWFALL (CM)	70.9	59.2	45.9	17.3	3.7	0.0	0.0	0.0	0.0	1.9	11.9	55.0	265.9
PRECIPITATION (MM)	126.7	101.5	110.6	90.2	97.4	81.4	87.6	85.5	87.3	95.5	117.4	129.9	1210.9

PUGWASH

CATEGORY	JAN	FEB	MAR	APR	MAY	JUN	JUL	AUG	SEP	OCT	NOV	DEC	YEAR
DAILY MAXIMUM (°C)	-1.8	-1.6	2.6	8.1	15.6	20.9	24.7	23.9	19.2	13.1	7.0	1.0	11.1
DAILY MINIMUM (°C)	-11.6	-11.1	-6.0	0.0	5.8	11.0	14.8	14.4	10.3	4.8	-0.1	-7.5	2.1
RAINFALL (MM)	52.4	28.5	42.4	65.7	84.8	77.5	79.5	85.6	92.7	98.7	93.5	62.4	863.6
SNOWFALL (CM)	46.2	41.8	38.6	14.4	1.2	0.0	0.0	0.0	0.0	0.0	7.7	38.8	188.7
PRECIPITATION (MM)	98.6	70.3	81.0	80.0	86.1	77.5	79.5	85.6	92.7	98.7	101.2	101.2	1052.2

SYDNEY

CATEGORY	JAN	FEB	MAR	APR	MAY	JUN	JUL	AUG	SEP	OCT	NOV	DEC	YEAR
DAILY MAXIMUM (°C)	-1.3	-1.9	1.5	6.1	12.9	18.9	23.0	22.7	18.3	12.2	6.8	1.6	10.1
DAILY MINIMUM (°C)	-10.0	-11.1	-6.9	-1.9	2.6	7.6	12.3	12.6	8.5	3.8	-0.2	-5.8	1.0
RAINFALL (MM)	82.4	66.7	88.4	103.7	100.1	92.6	86.8	93.1	113.4	143.8	134.4	107.6	1212.9
SNOWFALL (CM)	70.8	66.8	51.4	26.1	2.7	0.0	0.0	0.0	0.0	2.0	15.7	62.8	298.3
PRECIPITATION (MM)	151.5	132.1	138.9	130.4	102.9	92.6	86.8	93.1	113.4	146.0	149.7	167.5	1504.9

YARMOUTH

CATEGORY	JAN	FEB	MAR	APR	MAY	JUN	JUL	AUG	SEP	OCT	NOV	DEC	YEAR
DAILY MAXIMUM (°C)	1.0	0.8	4.1	8.7	13.8	17.9	20.6	21.0	17.8	13.1	8.3	3.6	10.9
DAILY MINIMUM (°C)	-7.0	-6.8	-3.4	1.1	5.4	9.4	12.4	12.7	9.6	5.1	1.3	-4.1	3.0
RAINFALL (MM)	84.2	65.2	84.1	89.6	97.7	94.2	84.5	74.4	99.1	107.9	123.2	98.7	1102.8
SNOWFALL (CM)	65.2	44.2	30.0	9.5	0.8	0.0	0.0	0.0	0.0	1.6	7.3	42.9	201.4
PRECIPITATION (MM)	136.1	100.8	113.5	98.9	98.5	94.2	84.5	74.4	99.1	109.6	129.9	134.7	1274.1

CHARLOTTETOWN

CATEGORY	JAN	FEB	MAR	APR	MAY	JUN	JUL	AUG	SEP	OCT	NOV	DEC	YEAR
DAILY MAXIMUM (°C)	-3.3	-3.3	0.9	6.7	14.1	19.6	23.2	22.6	18.0	11.8	5.7	-0.1	9.7
DAILY MINIMUM (°C)	-12.6	-12.4	-7.1	-1.4	4.0	9.6	13.8	13.5	9.1	3.8	-1.1	-8.1	0.9
RAINFALL (MM)	42.1	30.1	38.8	59.0	93.8	93.2	85.8	87.3	95.4	105.2	87.1	62.6	880.4
SNOWFALL (CM)	71.1	60.2	53.4	28.9	3.8	0.0	0.0	0.0	0.0	3.1	23.0	68.4	311.9
PRECIPITATION (MM)	106.4	85.5	91.8	87.8	97.7	93.2	85.8	87.3	95.4	108.6	110.8	123.1	1173.3

SUMMERSIDE

CATEGORY	JAN	FEB	MAR	APR	MAY	JUN	JUL	AUG	SEP	OCT	NOV	DEC	YEAR
DAILY MAXIMUM (°C)	-3.4	-3.0	1.2	6.7	14.0	19.6	23.6	22.9	18.0	11.9	5.6	-0.3	9.7
DAILY MINIMUM (°C)	-12.3	-11.7	-6.8	-1.1	4.7	10.2	14.5	14.2	9.8	4.4	-0.9	-8.0	1.4
RAINFALL (MM)	31.3	25.1	33.3	53.9	91.9	84.4	84.8	88.3	91.8	92.1	76.2	52.9	806.0
SNOWFALL (CM)	74.0	52.9	50.6	25.3	2.3	0.0	0.0	0.0	0.0	2.3	19.3	55.0	281.7
PRECIPITATION (MM)	100.1	75.1	83.8	79.7	94.0	84.4	84.8	88.3	91.7	94.5	96.7	105.0	1078.0

MARITIMES CLIMATE EXTREMES 1971–2000

(Adapted from the Meteorological Service of Canada data
as posted on the Environment Canada website)

BATHURST

MAXIMUM (°C)	36.5 ON JULY 4, 1983
MINIMUM (°C)	-36.1 ON JANUARY 12, 1976
DAILY RAINFALL (MM)	89.7 ON SEPTEMBER 9, 1969
DAILY SNOWFALL (CM)	70.0 ON DECEMBER 3, 1989
SNOW DEPTH (CM)	213.0 ON DECEMBER 28, 1978

KENTVILLE

MAXIMUM (°C)	37.8 ON AUGUST 12, 194▯
MINIMUM (°C)	-31.1 ON FEBRUARY 1, 1▯
DAILY RAINFALL (MM)	144.5 ON SEPTEMBER 22
DAILY SNOWFALL (CM)	53.3 ON JANUARY 5, 195▯
SNOW DEPTH (CM)	138.0 ON MARCH 19, 19▯

FERDERICTON

MAXIMUM (°C)	37.2 ON AUGUST 2, 1975
MINIMUM (°C)	-37.2 ON FEBRUARY 2, 1962
DAILY RAINFALL (MM)	148.6 ON AUGUST 5, 1989
DAILY SNOWFALL (CM)	78.0 ON DECEMBER 4, 1967
SNOW DEPTH (CM)	124.0 ON DECEMBER 28, 1970

PUGWASH

MAXIMUM (°C)	36.0 ON JULY 20, 1991
MINIMUM (°C)	-37.0 ON FEBRUARY 7, 1▯
DAILY RAINFALL (MM)	101.6 ON JULY 22, 1983
DAILY SNOWFALL (CM)	70.0 ON FEBRUARY 1, 19▯
SNOW DEPTH (CM)	110.0 ON FEBRUARY 6, 1▯

GRAND FALLS

MAXIMUM (°C)	33.9 ON JUNE 4, 1967
MINIMUM (°C)	-38.0 ON MARCH 1, 1982
DAILY RAINFALL (MM)	83.6 ON SEPTEMBER 9, 1969
DAILY SNOWFALL (CM)	48.0 ON JANUARY 3, 1986
SNOW DEPTH (CM)	70.0 ON JANUARY 31, 1991

SYDNEY

MAXIMUM (°C)	35.5 ON AUGUST 10, 20▯
MINIMUM (°C)	-27.3 ON FEBRUARY 8, 1▯
DAILY RAINFALL (MM)	128.8 ON AUGUST 17, 19▯
DAILY SNOWFALL (CM)	58.7 ON DECEMBER 21,
SNOW DEPTH (CM)	123.0 ON FEBRUARY 9,

MONCTON

MAXIMUM (°C)	37.2 ON AUGUST 12, 1944
MINIMUM (°C)	-32.2 ON JANUARY 14, 1957
DAILY RAINFALL (MM)	131.8 ON APRIL 1, 1962
DAILY SNOWFALL (CM)	83.0 ON FEBRUARY 1, 1992
SNOW DEPTH (CM)	168.0 ON DECEMBER 27, 1970

YARMOUTH

MAXIMUM (°C)	30.3 ON AUGUST 27, 19▯
MINIMUM (°C)	-23.6 ON FEBRUARY 7, 1▯
DAILY RAINFALL (MM)	172.5 ON OCTOBER 1, 1
DAILY SNOWFALL (CM)	50.8 ON MARCH 10, 19▯
SNOW DEPTH (CM)	83.0 ON JANUARY 18, 1

SAINT JOHN

MAXIMUM (°C)	34.4 ON AUGUST 22, 1976
MINIMUM (°C)	-36.7 ON FEBRUARY 11, 1948
DAILY RAINFALL (MM)	154.4 ON NOVEMBER 13, 1975
DAILY SNOWFALL (CM)	58.2 ON DECEMBER 12, 1960
SNOW DEPTH (CM)	102.0 ON FEBRUARY 25, 1963

CHARLOTTETOWN

MAXIMUM (°C)	34.4 ON AUGUST 12, 19▯
MINIMUM (°C)	-30.5 ON JANUARY 18,
DAILY RAINFALL (MM)	106.4 ON OCTOBER 10,
DAILY SNOWFALL (CM)	47.5 ON FEBRUARY 7, 1
SNOW DEPTH (CM)	156.0 ON FEBRUARY 13▯

HALIFAX

MAXIMUM (°C)	35.0 ON AUGUST 1, 1995
MINIMUM (°C)	-28.5 ON JANUARY 31, 1993
DAILY RAINFALL (MM)	218.2 ON AUGUST 15, 1971
DAILY SNOWFALL (CM)	47.5 ON DECEMBER 24, 1970
SNOW DEPTH (CM)	94.0 ON JANUARY 24, 1971

SUMMERSIDE

MAXIMUM (°C)	33.3 ON AUGUST 13, 19▯
MINIMUM (°C)	-29.9 ON JANUARY 18,
DAILY RAINFALL (MM)	111.8 ON AUGUST 13, 1▯
DAILY SNOWFALL (CM)	53.6 ON JANUARY 1, 19▯
SNOW DEPTH (CM)	114.0 ON FEBRUARY 22▯

HARDINESS ZONE MAP

HARDINESS ZONES

	2a
	2b
	3a
	3b
	4a
	4b
	5a
	5b
	6a

FROST DATE MAPS

LAST SPRING FROST DATES

	MAY 1 – MAY 15
	MAY 15 – JUNE 1
	JUNE 1 – JUNE 15
	JUNE 15 – JULY 1

FIRST FALL FROST DATES

	AUGUST 15 – SEPTEMBER 1
	SEPTEMBER 1 – SEPTEMBER 15
	SEPTEMBER 15 – OCTOBER 1
	OCTOBER 1 – OCTOBER 15
	OCTOBER 15 – NOVEMBER 1
	NOVEMBER 1 – NOVEMBER 15

JANUARY

*Now is the time for planning and
dreaming of the distant summer
and the garden yet to be.*

JANUARY

Avoid using chemical de-icers because they are harmful to lawns and garden plants, and they add to the salt problem in areas affected by salt-laden wind and spray.

Instead of recycling your Christmas tree, cut it up and use the branches as a mulch to shelter low-growing shrubs and groundcovers.

One of the flowers you might dream of adding to your garden in spring is the beautiful hybrid tea 'Loving Memory' (*left*). This zone 5 rose will flourish in many Maritime gardens. Cotoneaster (*right*)

In most years, the garden is blanketed in snow in January, but many Maritime gardens are just as likely to be bare and exposed to fluctuations in temperature. South-facing walls are always warmer than other areas of the garden. Snow melts most quickly here, leaving plants vulnerable to the stressful cycles of heat and cold. A good, thick fall mulch proves to be extremely valuable in a snowless year or a snowless area.

THINGS TO DO

January is one of the hardest months for the garden and the easiest for the gardener.

The ice storms and freezing rain that commonly occur during our winters can damage plants, though in warmer weather they should spring back to normal. Annual pruning promotes a compact form that resists ice damage.

Don't forget to top up your bird-feeders regularly. Feeding the birds encourages them to keep visiting in summer when they will help keep your insect pest populations under control.

Snow is the garden's best friend. Pile clean snow on snowless garden beds to insulate them against the wind and cold. Some people refer to this as 'snow farming.'

JANUARY

Avoid placing houseplants in hot or cold drafts

Order gardening and seed catalogues to look through even if you don't start your own seeds.

Ice fishers: save a bag of smelt or tommy co... in the freezer. Put one next to each potato ey... next spring for a great natural fertilizer.

Begonias (*left*) can be brought indoors in f... and kept as houseplants in a sunny locatio... through the winter. Peony-flowered poppie... (*top and bottom right*); Iceland poppies (*centre right*)

Gently brush snow off the branches of evergreens such as cedars, but leave any ice that forms to melt naturally. The weight of the snow or ice can permanently bend flexible branches, but more damage is done trying to remove ice than is done through its weight.

Choose and order seeds for early starting. Sort through the seeds you have, test them for viability and throw out any that don't germinate or that you won't grow. Trade seeds with gardening friends.

Get lawn mowers and other power tools serviced now. They will be ready for use in spring, and you may get a better price before the spring rush.

Annual poppy seeds are easy to collect and share. Pick seedheads when they are dry, and shake the fine seed on open ground from August to December for flowers next year.

To test older seeds for viability, place 10 seeds between two layers of moist paper towel and put them in a sealed container. Keep the paper evenly dampened but not too wet. Seeds may rot if the paper towel is too moist. Check each day to see if the seeds have sprouted. If fewer than half the seeds have sprouted after two weeks, buy new ones.

JANUARY

Reduce watering of houseplants because most need less water during winter.

To make a rustic suet holder, bore large holes in a short, round log, hung vertically. Fill holes with a peanut butter and bacon grease mix. Birds love it.

The datura (*left*) is an elegant, exotic-looking plant that produces large, showy, scented flowers. Daturas must be brought indoors in the winter or left to die with the annuals. Coleus (*top right*); English ivy topiary (*bottom right*)

Clean the foliage of your house-plants. When light levels are low, it is important for plants to be able to use whatever light is available. As a bonus, you might help reduce insect populations because their eggs will likely be wiped off along with the dust.

Check houseplants regularly for common indoor pests such as whiteflies, scale insects, spider mites and mealybugs.

GARDEN DESIGN

As you look out your windows at the frozen yard, think about what could make your garden look attractive in winter. Features such as birdbaths, ponds, benches, decks and winding pathways improve the look and function of your garden year-round. Persistent fruit or seedheads, unusual bark and branch patterns, evergreens and colourfully stemmed shrubs also provide winter interest.

Most indoor plants will benefit from increased humidity levels. Place pots on a tray of pebbles. If you add water to the pebbles when needed, you will increase the humidity through evaporation but prevent water-logged roots.

JANUARY

January is a great time for garden planning. In winter, the bones of the garden are laid bare, so you can take a good look at the garden's overall structure.

Give pot-bound houseplants a boost—and make them look better too—by repotting them into larger pots every year or two.

Rosehips (*left*), spiral topiary, the bright berries of viburnum (*top left and right*), the winged seeds of amur maple (*centre right*), and the curving branches of Japanese maple (*bottom right*) add interest to the garden in winter.

Plants that add variety to a winter garden:

- Clematis (*Clematis*): fuzzy seed-heads
- Corkscrew Hazel (*Corylus*): twisted and contorted branches
- Cotoneaster (*Cotoneaster*): persistent red berries
- Dogwood (*Cornus*): red, purple or yellow stems
- Highbush Cranberry (*Viburnum trilobum*): bright red berries
- Maple (*Acer ginnala*, *A. palmatum*): attractive bark and branching patterns
- Shrub Rose (*Rosa*): brightly coloured hips
- Topiary: sculpted trees, many species, in spiral, pompom and clipped standard shapes
- Weeping trees such as Peatree (*Caragana*), Birch (*Betula*), Mulberry (*Morus*): striking form
- White cedar (*Thuja*), False Cypress (*Chamaecyparis*) or Juniper (*Juniperus*): evergreen branches
- Winged Euonymus (*Euonymus alatus*): corky ridges on the branches

JANUARY

*Imagine the garden you'd like to have,
and keep this notebook and your diagrams
at hand so you can jot down ideas
as they come to you.*

*The gorgeous blue of Colorado spruce is a
surface pigment that may get weathered away
during winter. June's flush of growth brings
new steel blue needles.*

Woody evergreens,
such as white cedar
(*left*), upright juniper
(*top right*) and white
spruce (*far right*), add
interesting texture and
rich green colour to a
sometimes monotonous
winter landscape.

PROBLEM AREAS IN THE GARDEN

Keep track of these potential problem areas in your garden:

- windswept areas: perhaps a tree, shrub or hedge could be added next summer to provide shelter
- snowfree areas: places where the snow is always quick to melt are poor choices for very tender plants, which benefit most from the protection of the snow
- snowbound areas: places where the snow is slowest to melt provide the most protection to plants but stay frozen longest in spring, making them poor locations for spring-flowering plants
- waterlogged areas: places where water pools or is slow to drain during extended wet periods are best reserved for plants that tolerate their roots being wet
- dry areas: places that rarely get wet and drain quickly when they do should be used for drought-tolerant plants

Spruce are widely grown, and new varieties are available almost every gardening season. They are well suited to cold winters, and some, such as the Colorado blue spruce (*left*), provide wonderful blue-green colour against brilliant white snow.

FEBRUARY

The longer days and occasional warm
spells turn our thoughts to the
upcoming gardening season.

FEBRUARY

Keep a birdfeeder stocked with niger (thistle seed) all winter and goldfinches may stick around. Siskins and redpolls like them, too.

Keep an eye out for low spots and puddles in garden beds. 'Wet feet' kills more perennials than extreme cold in winter. Raise these areas next spring for better drainage.

Colourful little crabapples often remain on the branches of the tree through winter, a reminder of the beautiful blossoms to come in spring (*left and top right*). Flowering crabapp trees in spring (*bottom right*)

Groundhog Day is a teaser for Maritime gardeners. By February we all want winter to be over soon, but more often than not, the cold and snow stay around. Gardening can get under way, however. Finish ordering plants and seeds from catalogues and gather other supplies for indoor seeding, such as containers, soil, amendments and lights.

THINGS TO DO

February is another month with few tasks, but preparations can be made now that will keep things moving smoothly once the season kicks into high gear.

Check shrubs and trees for storm-damaged branches, and remove them using proper pruning techniques.

Cut branches of flowering shrubs, such as forsythia, crabapple and cherry, to bring indoors. Placed in a bright location in a vase of water, they will begin to flower, giving you a taste of spring in winter.

FEBRUARY

Three excellent houseplants for low light areas are spider plant (Chlorophytum), Janet Craig compact Dracaena (Dracaena) and umbrella tree (Schefflera).

Continue to check for insect pests on your houseplants.

Thoroughly clean empty planters, containers and seed trays to get them ready for spring planting.

Don't forget your fish out there in the cold! Keep a small hole in the pond ice open to let gases out and oxygen in. A small pump on the bottom of the pond aimed upwards keeps a spot open all winter.

Dianthus (*left*), browallia (*top left*), bellflower (*far right*) and begonia (*near right*) are plants you can start from seed in February.

Some slower growing annual and perennial flowers should be started in late February:

- Amethyst Flower (*Browallia*)
- Baby's Breath (*Gypsophila*)
- Begonia (*Begonia*)
- Bellflower (*Campanula*)
- Dusty Miller (*Senecio*)
- Geranium (*Pelargonium*)
- Lady's Mantle (*Alchemilla*)
- Pansy (*Viola*)
- Pinks (*Dianthus*)

Starting plants from seed is a great way to propagate a large number of plants at a relatively low cost. You can grow plants you can't find at any garden centre and get a jump-start on the growing season.

FEBRUARY

Pond lovers, bring your hobby inside for winter with an aquarium. Start small (and less expensive) goldfish and koi inside to put in your pond when they get big.

Check to see if any of the tubers or bulbs you are storing indoors have started sprouting. Pot them and keep them in a bright location once they do.

Many varieties of dahlia (*left*) can be star[t] from seed in March for transplanting a[fter] the danger of frost has passed. Oran[ge] tree as a houseplant (*top left*); fresh herbs growing in a greenhouse in winter (*centre right*); seed tray, pot[ting] soil and spray mister for indoor seeding (*bottom right*)

STARTING SEEDS

To start seeds, you'll need
- pots, trays or peat pots
- sterile seed-starting mix
- plastic bags or tray covers to keep the seedbed humid
- spray bottle or watering can with sprinkler attachment
- heat mat (optional)

Seedlings will be weak and floppy if they don't get enough light. Consider purchasing a fluorescent or other grow light (*above*) to provide extra illumination for them.

Styrofoam meat trays make economical seed-starting trays. Seeds sprinkled on moist perlite and covered with plastic wrap germinate quickly. Lift wrap when seed leaves form (one to two weeks) and transplant.

Tips for growing healthy seedlings:
Transplant seedlings to individual containers once they have three or four true leaves to prevent crowding.
Space plants so that the leaves do not overshadow those of neighbouring plants.
Grow seedlings in moderate temperatures away from direct heat.
Provide air circulation with a small fan to keep foliar diseases from starting.
Don't fertilize young seedlings until the seed leaves (the first leaves to appear) have begun to shrivel; then fertilize with a weak fertilizer once a week.

FEBRUARY

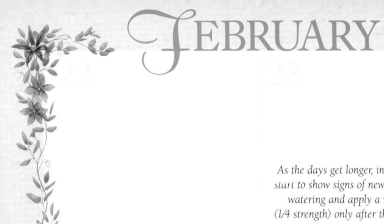

As the days get longer, indoor plants may start to show signs of new growth. Increase watering and apply a weak fertilizer (1/4 strength) only after they begin to grow.

Do most of your indoor seeding in March and April so that you'll have sturdy transplants ready by the time the last frost has come and gone in spring (late May to early June). For guidance, see the seed-starting notices in March and April.

Hardy in zones 2–9, the Martin Frobisher shrub rose (*left*) was the first rose in the Explorer series. It blooms repeatedly from early summer to fall, producing fragrant, double, pale pink flowers reminiscent of old roses.

SEED STARTING TIPS

- Moisten the soil before you fill the containers.
- Firm the soil down in the containers, but don't pack it too tightly.
- Leave seeds that require light for germination uncovered.
- Plant large seeds individually by poking a hole in the soil with the tip of a pen or pencil and then dropping the seed in the hole.
- Spread small seeds evenly across the soil surface, then lightly cover with more soil mix.
- To spread small seeds, place them in the crease of a folded piece of paper and gently tap the bottom of the fold to roll them onto the soil (*top right*).
- Mix very tiny seeds, like those of begonia, with very fine sand before planting to spread them out more evenly.
- Plant only one type of seed in each container. Some seeds will germinate before others, and it is difficult to keep both seeds and seedlings happy in the same container.
- Cover pots or trays of seeds with clear plastic to keep them moist (*right*).
- Seeds do not need bright, direct light to germinate and can be kept in an out-of-the-way place until they begin to sprout.
- After germination, and once seedlings start to emerge, moisten the soil with a hand-held spray mister when it begins to dry out.
- Keep seedlings in a bright location to reduce stretching, and remove plastic cover.

To prevent seedlings from damping-off, always use a sterile soil mix, thoroughly clean containers before using them, maintain good air circulation around seedlings and keep the soil moist, not soggy.

FEBRUARY

Envision the garden you want rather than the one you have by designing your own layout (*example below*). Garden design can be as simple as planting a container to display on your patio or deck, or as complex as creating beds and borders or building shelters, walkways or a pond (*opposite page*).

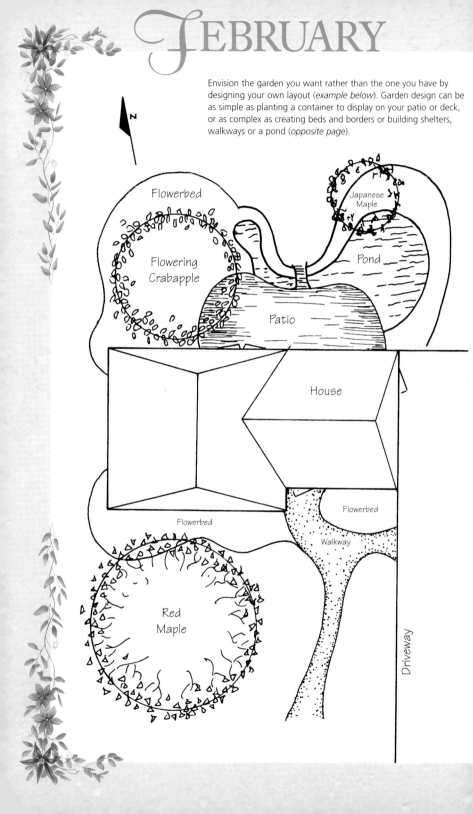

N

Flowerbed

Flowering
Crabapple

Japanese
Maple

Pond

Patio

House

Flowerbed

Walkway

Flowerbed

Red
Maple

Driveway

GARDEN PLANNING

Using graph paper, plot out the existing yard and house:

- Put in trees, shrubs and other solid structural elements. If you remember where the flowerbeds are, add those as well. Garden beds can be added later if you're not sure. Make copies and use them to keep track of your plans.
- Create a master plan and then sub-plans so you can keep track of the changes you'd like to make each year.
- Make another plan of just your vegetable garden, if you have one, so you can plan and keep track of crop rotations.

MARCH

Expect the unexpected in March. Our gardens
can be under a blanket of snow one day
and showing the first signs of spring the next.

MARCH

1

2

Prune any growth that was damaged over winter off your trees and shrubs (see p. 58).

3

4

The single most important thing you can do when planting is to make sure you have the right plant in the right location. Consider the mature size of the plant and its cultural requirements.

5

6

When pruning larger limbs, look for the branch collar (ring of bark at the base) and prune just outside the collar to ensure proper healing. Leave the pruned area exposed to dry and heal—do not apply tree paint or tar.

7

When designing your garden, consider planting a fast-growing, drought-tolerant elder (*left and near right*). The elder's showy foliage adds colour and texture to landscape, and its edible berries can be made into je or wine, or left for the birds.

Early warm spells lure us out to see what's sprouting. Catkins and pussy willows begin to swell, hellebores open from beneath the melting snow and snowdrops begin the long parade of spring bulbs. Just when we think winter is over, a late snowfall blankets the garden and we go back to planning.

THINGS TO DO

The first few tasks of spring get us out in the garden in March.

Days can be warm enough so that some plants start sprouting. Keep snow piled on beds or top up mulches to protect tender plants from the freezing nights.

Prune red-twig dogwoods (*above*) anytime after snowmelt, but wait to prune spring-bloomers like the native pagoda dogwood (*top*) until they finish blooming.

MARCH

*As the snow melts, start clearing up
the debris in your yard, such as leaves,
sticks, garbage and animal droppings.*

SEEDS TO START NOW
leeks, onions

*Prune late-flowering shrubs (July or later)
and shrubs grown for colourful young growth
(see p. 58 for tips).*

As soon as the snow begins to melt in
spring, the leaves of the bergenia becor
visible and are quickly followed by its
pretty magenta flowers (*left*).
Spirea (*top right*); hardy kiwi
(*centre right*); big-leaf
hydrangea (*bottom right*).
Bigleaf hydrangeas should b
given a sheltered spot and
winter mulch.

Keep off your lawn when it is frozen, bare of snow and/or very wet to avoid damaging the grass or compacting the soil.

Apply horticultural oil (also called dormant oil), used to control over-wintering insects, to trees, shrubs and vines, before the buds swell. Follow the directions carefully to avoid harming plants and beneficial insects.

Plants to prune in spring:
- Butterfly Bush (*Buddleia davidii*)
- Golden or Purple-leafed Elder (*Sambucus*)
- Hardy Kiwi (*Actinidia arguta*)
- Hydrangea (*Hydrangea*)
- Japanese Spirea (*Spirea japonica*)
- Potentilla (*Potentilla*)
- Red-twig Dogwood (*Cornus* spp.)
- Spirea (*Spiraea*)

MARCH

15

SEEDS TO START NOW
alyssum, candytuft, cosmos, delphinium,
foxglove, impatiens, salvia, sweet william

16

Traditional maple-tapping season starts now and
continues for a month or so. Twenty taps, one or
two per mature sugar maple tree, will yield a
gallon or more of delicious syrup per season.

17

18

More houseplants will start growing
in response to longer days; increase
watering and fertilize sparingly.

19

20

21

Bigleaf (or *macrophylla*) hydrangea (*left*) is
popular shrub that needs a protected site
and moist soil. If planted early enough in
spring, clematis (*top left*) flowers the first
summer.

PLANTING IN SPRING

Early spring is prime planting time. Trees, shrubs, vines and perennials often establish most quickly if planted just as they are about to break dormancy. Plan now what you will want to move, divide and plant as soon as you can work the ground in April.

Avoid using horticultural oil on blue-needled evergreens, such as blue spruce (*above and below*). The treatment takes the blue off the existing needles, though the new needles will be blue.

MARCH

22

23

Before doing any digging, call your utility companies to locate any buried wires, cables or pipes. Doing so prevents injury and saves time and money.

SEEDS TO START NOW
carnation, lobelia, feverfew, chrysanthemum

24

25

Don't plant vigorous spreaders in rock gardens with tiny alpine plants or large shrubs right next to walkways. Choose the plant that best fits the location.

26

27

To keep secateurs sharp, use a round file on the bevelled edge of the blade only. Four or five strokes should do the job.

28

Rhododendrons (*left*) thrive in sheltered locations and must be planted in moist, fertile, acidic and well-drain soil to do well. Rhododendrons are sensitive to high pH, salinity and extreme winter expose and will not grow well if these conditions are present. Flower quince (*top right*); goat's be (*bottom right*)

A few things to keep in mind when planting your garden:

- Never work with your soil when it is very wet or very dry.

- Avoid planting during the hottest, sunniest part of the day. Choose an overcast day, or plant early or late in the day.

- Prepare your soil before you plant to avoid damaging roots later.

- Get your new plants into the ground as soon as possible when you get them home. Roots can get hot and dry out quickly in containers. Keep plants in a shady spot if you must wait to plant them.

- Plants are happiest when planted at the same depth they have always grown at. Trees, in particular, can be killed by too deep a planting.

- Remove containers before planting. Plastic and fibre pots restrict root growth and prevent plants from becoming established.

- Plants should be well watered when they are newly planted. Watering deeply and infrequently will encourage the strongest root growth.

- Check the root zone before watering. The soil surface may appear dry when the roots are still moist.

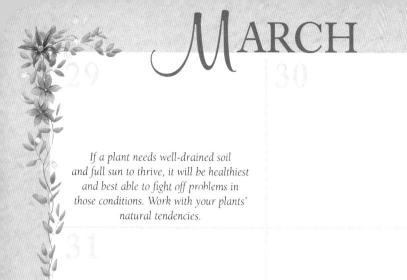

MARCH

29

30

If a plant needs well-drained soil and full sun to thrive, it will be healthiest and best able to fight off problems in those conditions. Work with your plants' natural tendencies.

31

The splendid yellow shrub rose 'Morden Sunrise' (*below*) works well in cold and mild climates. Flower colour intensifies in cooler temperatures and becomes softer and paler in hot weather.

Harden annuals and perennials off before planting them by gradually exposing them to longer periods of time outside. Doing so gives your plants time to adapt to outdoor weather conditions and reduces the chance of transplant shock. Hardening off allows plants to adapt to outdoor conditions and reduces transplant shock. Hardy perennials can be planted by late April and annuals by late May.

Trees less than 1.5 m (5') tall do not need staking unless they are in a very windy location. Unstaked trees develop stronger root systems.

Remove only dead and damaged branches when planting trees or shrubs, and let the plant establish itself for at least one year before you begin any formative pruning. Plants need all the branches and leaves they have when they are trying to get established.

planting a balled-and-burlapped tree

planting a bare-root tree

staking a tree properly

APRIL

Cool, wet weather prevails, but the garden
continues to awaken, sprout and flower.
Spring is almost here.

APRIL

1

aster, celery, pepper, petunia, pinks, snapdragon, zinnia

2

Plant trees, shrubs and vines once the soil can be worked.

3

4

Check your power tools, such as the lawn mower, and have them serviced if you didn't do it over winter.

5

6

7

The columbine (*left*) is a beautiful flower that some say resembles a bird in flight. Its jewel-like colours herald the coming of summer. *Opposite page, clockwise from top left:* primroses; tulips; Bethlehem sage (*Pulmonaria saccharata* 'Mrs Moon'), all early bloomers

Frequent and early trips to the garden centre give you an opportunity to buy spring-flowering plants and those in limited supply. Regular trips through the season allow you to see what's in bloom at different times so you can create a garden of long-lasting floral displays.

Though winter seems to have passed for most gardeners, it doesn't yet feel warm enough to be spring. Old snowbanks take forever to melt. Fog, rain and even a late spring flurry hold off the warmer weather. Green shoots emerge and call us to the garden, but only the truly devoted venture forth. The rest of us feel assured that warm days are just around the corner and that the tidying can wait just a bit longer.

April

8

9

Pull back mulch from sprouting plants, but keep mulch or a sheet handy to cover plants up when frost is expected.

10

11

Clean up the garden. Rake debris off lawns and prune back old perennial growth.

12

13

14

Consider planting daylilies (*left*) this spring. Though each bloom lasts only a day, these hardy perennials are easy going, prolific and versatile, and come in an almost infinite variety of forms, sizes and colours. Magnolia (*top right*); California poppies (*bottom right*)

THINGS TO DO

Gear up for raking, digging, planting and pruning. We begin the hard work that will let us sit back and enjoy the garden once summer arrives.

Bring garden tools out of storage and examine them for rust or other damage. Clean and sharpen them if you didn't before you put them away in fall.

Store any plants you have purchased or started indoors in as bright a location as possible. You may begin to harden them off by placing them outdoors for a short period on warmer days.

Avoid working your soil until it has thawed and dried out a bit. It's dry enough when you can make a soil ball that will crumble apart again when squeezed.

Ever considered creating your own bonsai? It's a great activity for a rainy day. The best plant to start with is a one- or two-gallon potted Japanese garden juniper. Prune away excess branches to reveal the twisted trunk structure: instant bonsai. Get a textbook for a detailed how-to.

Seeds sown directly into the garden may take longer to germinate than those planted indoors, but the resulting plants, such as California poppies (*right*), will be stronger.

APRIL

15

16

SEEDS TO START NOW
*coleus, dwarf dahlia, herbs, lavatera,
marigold, tomato*

17

18

19

20

*Divide perennials that bloom in summer or
later, such as asters, daylilies and sedums as
soon as plants exhibit spring growth.*

21

Clematis such as C. 'Gravetye Beauty' (*left*) are popula
perennial vines with beautiful, showy flowers in
many shapes and sizes. By planting a variety of ther
you can have clematis in bloom from spring to fall.
Opposite page, clockwise from top left: C. 'Hagley
Hybrid'; *C. integrifolia; C. viticella* 'Etoile Violette'

Remove mulch from perennials and trim back and clear away any of last year's growth. Be careful not to damage new shoots.

Clear away any of the annuals or vegetables that didn't make it to the compost pile last fall.

By the end of the month, you will have a good idea of what has been damaged or killed back over winter, and you can trim or remove plants as needed.

Cool, wet spring weather can cause drought-loving plants to rot. Improve soil drainage through the addition of organic matter and by raising bed height.

Dwarf Alberta spruce doesn't like hot sun and may burn or get spider mites if planted in a sheltered, south-facing location. Plant it in a breezy, partly shaded spot.

APRIL

22

SEEDS TO START NOW
*vegetables in the cabbage family,
hollyhocks, lettuce*

23

Repot houseplants if needed.

24

*Branched twigs make great natural supports
for leaning houseplants such as
umbrella tree, dracaena and jade plant.
They blend in perfectly and work
for outdoor flowers, too.*

25

26

27

28

You can depend on aubretia (*left*) to put
on a great floral show in spring. *Opposit
page, clockwise from top right:*
pruning a flowering crabapple;
pompom juniper; formally
pruned yew hedge and
white cedar

PRUNING

Prune trees and shrubs to maintain their health and attractive shape, increase the quality and yield of fruit, control and direct growth and create interesting plant forms.

Once you learn how to prune plants correctly, it is an enjoyable garden task. There are many good books available on the topic of pruning. Two are listed at the back of this book. If you are unsure about pruning, take a pruning course, often offered by garden centres, botanical gardens and adult education programs.

Start pruning when your shrubs are young. That way it's an easy task, and you'll learn as the plant grows how it responds to your pruning.

APRIL

29   30

Opposite page, clockwise from top left: climbing rose with support; espalier; proper secateur orientation

PRUNING TIPS

- Prune at the right time of year. Trees and shrubs that flower before June, usually on the previous year's wood, should be pruned after they have flowered. Trees and shrubs that flower after June, usually on new growth, can be pruned in spring.

- Use the correct tool for the size of branch to be removed: secateurs, or hand pruners, for growth up to 2 cm (¾") in diameter; long-handled loppers for growth up to 4 cm (1½") in diameter; or a pruning saw for growth up to about 15 cm (6") in diameter.

- Always use clean and sharp tools.

- Always use secateurs or loppers with the blade side towards the plant and the hook towards the part to be removed.

thinning cuts

Thin trees and shrubs to promote the growth of younger, healthier branches. Doing so rejuvenates a plant. Thinning out longer branches will control size and shape.

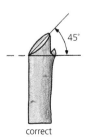

correct

too low

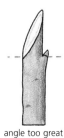

angle too great

too high

When pruning, avoid the following:
- Don't leave stubs. Whether you are cutting off a large branch or deadheading a lilac, always cut back to a joint. Branches should be removed to the branch collar, and smaller growth should be cut back to a bud or branch union. There is no absolute set angle for pruning. Each plant should be pruned according to its individual needs.
- Never use pruning paint or paste. Trees have a natural ability to create a barrier between living and dead wood. Painting over a cut impairs this ability.

Never try to remove a tree or large branch by yourself. Have someone help you, or hire a professional to do it.

Don't top trees. It's bad for their health and makes them look ugly.

Always hire an ISA (International Society of Arboriculture) certified professional to remove branches on trees growing near power lines or other hazardous areas, especially if they could damage a building, fence or car if they were to fall. Branches and trees are usually much heavier than anticipated and can do a lot of damage if they fall in the wrong place.

MAY

The promise of spring is fulfilled with
the sprouting and blooming of May, and
winter becomes a distant memory.

MAY

Move or divide any perennials that didn't
have enough space last summer.

Start new garden beds or expand
and improve old ones.

Time to clean your pond. Drain the water,
keeping fish in a large cooler of pond water;
hand pick, flush and pump out leaves and
debris; divide lilies and other plants; install the
pump; refill the pond and return your fish.

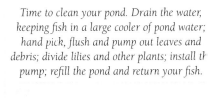

The Japanese anemone or windflower (*left*) is
an attractive plant at all stages. Some varieties
bloom in spring while others reserve their lovely
display for fall. Saucer magnolia (*top right*) flowers
in mid- to late spring; the combination of tulips and
pansies (*bottom right*) makes an interesting colour
and height contrast in a spring flowerbed.

May weather is unpredictable, one year warm and sunny and the next cold and wet. In a typical May, bulbs are blooming, peonies poke up their red and green spears and spring-flowering trees like magnolia and crabapple burst forth in a riot of colour. Even the most devoted lawn lover knows that spring is truly here when the first dandelion of spring, tucked up against a south wall, opens its fuzzy face to the sun.

THINGS TO DO

A new gardening season awaits, one where we haven't forgotten to weed or water, where all our plants are properly spaced and well staked and where no insects have chewed any leaves. Now is the time to finish tidying up the garden, prepare the garden beds and get the planting done.

MAY

snapdragons, cleome (spiderflower)

Begin to harden off any houseplants you plan to move outdoors for summer.

Work compost into your garden beds and fork them over, removing weeds as you go, to prepare them for planting later in the month.

A traditional garden favourite, sweet pea *(left)* are easy to grow from seed in spring. They sprout quickly and have sweetly scented blooms that can be cut often for fragrant indoor bouquets. *Opposite page, clockwise from top left,* phlox, cabbage, rocket larkspur and nigella can be planted before the last spring frost.

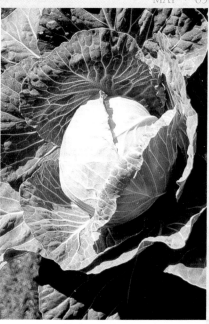

Many plants prefer to grow in cool weather and can be started outside well before the last frost. These seeds can be planted as soon as the soil can be worked:

- Bachelor's Buttons (*Centaurea cyanus*)
- Cabbage (*Brassica oleracea*)
- Calendula (*Calendula officinalis*)
- California Poppy (*Eschscholzia californica*)
- Godetia (*Clarkia amoena*)
- Kale (*Brassica napus*)
- Love-in-a-Mist (*Nigella damascena*)
- Peas (*Pisum sativum*)
- Phlox (*Phlox drummondii*)
- Poppy (*Papaver rhoeas*)
- Potato (*Solanum tuberosum*)
- Rocket Larkspur (*Consolida ajacis*)
- Spinach (*Spinacea oleracea*)
- Sweet Pea (*Lathyrus odoratus*)
- Swiss Chard (*Beta vulgaris*)

ou can sow many seeds and lants early if you use row covers) warm up your vegetable beds.

MAY

cucumbers, squash, pumpkins, melons

Continue to harden off your early-started seedlings and purchased plants so they will be ready to plant outside as soon as the weather is warm enough.

When planning your vegetable garden, consider planting extra to donate to a local food bank or homeless shelter. Even if you just end up with extra zucchini and tomatoes, they can be put to good use.

Wait until this late date to seed heat-loving plants indoors to ensure vigorous transplants and warm soil and weather.

Plant a sunny spring flower such as doronicum (*left*) with tulips and forget-me-nots to create a cheerful May display.

It is possible to have a healthy, attractive organic lawn. Grass is an extremely competitive plant, capable of fighting off invasions by weeds, pests and diseases without the use of chemicals. Watering with compost tea encourages a healthy lawn.

Accept that grass will not grow everywhere. Grass requires plenty of sun and regular moisture. Many trees and buildings provide too much shade and don't allow enough water to get to the soil for grass to grow successfully. Use mulch or other groundcovers in areas where you have trouble growing grass. When selecting trees to plant in the lawn, choose ones that will provide only light shade and that will tolerate sharing a limited water supply with the grass, or have a grass-free zone extending from the base of the tree to the dripline.

Lawns need very little water to remain green. Watering deeply and infrequently will encourage deep roots that are not easily damaged during periods of drought. Generally, 2.5 cm (1") of water a week keeps grass green. Deeper topsoil (15 cm or 6" or more) with higher organic content needs less watering, if any.

The last frost in the Maritimes usually comes by late May, depending on the year and where you garden. In a warm year, when the nights stay above freezing even early in the month, you can try a few tender plants, such as tomatoes. If there are no more frosts, you will gain several weeks on the growing season. In a cool year you may have to wait until the end of May or the beginning of June before planting to give the soil more time to warm before planting tender heat-lovers such as squash, peppers and beans (*left*).

MAY

Leave several strong stems of asparagus uncut per plant to ensure future strength.

De-thatch lawns in spring if the thatch layer is deeper than 2 cm (³/₄"). Hardware stores carry simple attachments to make your lawnmower a de-thatching aid.

To restore bare spots in your lawn, loosen turf sprinkle grass seed and cover with compost.

With their wide variety of leaf shapes, sizes and colours, hosta (*left*) are a popular addition to shaded Maritime gardens.

TURFGRASS

Turfgrass aficionados are having a
hard time these days. Many cities
have banned pesticide use on
lawns, and summer water bans
leave turf dry and crisp during hot
spells. Alternative groundcovers
and xeriscapes are being hailed as
the way of the future, but there are
positives to turfgrasses that make
them worth keeping. Lawns effi-
ciently filter pollutants out of run-
off water, prevent soil erosion,
retain moisture, cool the air and
resist drought.

Although lawns require a layer of
thatch to improve wear tolerance,
reduce compaction and insulate
against weather extremes, too thick a
thatch layer can prevent water
absorption, make the grass suscep-
ble to heat, drought and cold and
encourage pest and disease problems.

May-blooming flowers (*clockwise
from top left*): some irises bloom in
early spring; forget-me-nots flower
in spring, set seed and go
dormant; rockcress and creeping
phlox flowers attract bees and
butterflies in spring and look
exceptional in rock gardens.

MAY

Start planting your vegetable garden now. All crops but heat lovers (e.g., beans, squash, tomatoes, peppers) are safe to sow or transplant.

Forget-me-nots (*left*), rockcress (*top right*) and bergenia (*bottom right*) are easy-to-grow, reliable bloomers and perfect for beginner gardeners.

Here are some tips for maintaining a healthy, organic lawn:

- Aerate your lawn in spring, after active growth begins, to relieve compaction and allow water and air to move freely through the soil.
- Feed the soil, not the plants. Organic fertilizers or compost will encourage a healthy population of soil microbes. These work with roots to provide plants with nutrients and to fight off attacks by pests and diseases. Raise low pH to about 7.0 by adding lime in fall or spring. This helps control weeds, which prefer acidic (sour) soil. Apply an organic fertilizer in late spring after you aerate the lawn and in fall just as the grass goes dormant.
- Keep lawn mowed to a height of 5–7 cm (2–3"). The remaining leaf blade shades the ground, reducing moisture loss and keeping roots cooler. Mowing less often keeps grass healthier and better able to out-compete weeds.

- Grass clippings should be left on the lawn to return their nutrients to the soil and add organic matter. Mowing your lawn once a week or as often as needed during the vigorous growing season will ensure that the clippings decompose quickly.
- Healthy grass out-competes most weeds. Remove weeds by hand. If you must use chemicals, apply them only to the weeds. Chemical herbicides disrupt the balance of soil microbes and are not necessary to have a healthy lawn.

JUNE

The long, warm days
of summer are with us, and the
garden flourishes.

JUNE

Finish planting tender transplants such as pumpkins, tomatoes, begonias and coleus.

Remove dead flowers from plants growing in tubs, window-boxes and hanging baskets. Deadheading encourages more flowering and keeps displays looking tidy.

Heat-loving plants such as beans and marigolds germinate quickly in warm soil. Direct sow early in June.

Deepen and define bed edges with an edger, hoe and grass shears.

Cranesbill geraniums (*left*) are charming late-spring perennials with attractive foliage. The leaves of some varieties emit a lemon-mint scent. *Clockwise from top left:* moonbean coreopsis and black-eyed Susan; daylilies and phlox; daylilies planted en masse serve as a screen.

In June, the grass is green, flower-beds are filling, and perennials, trees and shrubs are blooming. We watch as seeds germinate and leaves unfold. The fear of frost is behind us, and the soil is warm enough for even the most tender plants. Rain is usually plentiful in June, but in a dry year, newly planted annuals and perennials may need supplemental watering until they become established.

THINGS TO DO

June is the month to finish up the planting and begin general garden maintenance.

Stake plants (peonies, delphiniums) before they fill in if you haven't already done so.

Apply mulch to shrub, perennial and vegetable beds. Doing so will shade the roots and reduce the amount of water the plants will require in drier areas.

Goldfish actively graze algae off rocks. They do not need extra food, which pollutes the water and makes it cloudy with floating algae.

JUNE

Prune early-flowering shrubs that have finished flowering to encourage the development of young shoots that will bear flowers the following year.

Identify the insects you find in your garden. You may be surprised to find out how many are beneficial.

Despite the delicate look of its satiny flowers godetia (*left*) enjoys the cooler summer weather of the Maritimes. *Opposite page, clockwise from top left:* bee balm; black-eyed Susans mixed with purple cone-flower; purple coneflower; catmint

Perennials to pinch back in June:

- Artemisia (*Artemisia* spp.)
- Bee Balm (*Monarda didyma*)
- Black-eyed Susan (*Rudbeckia* spp.)
- Catmint (*Nepeta* hybrids)
- Purple Coneflower (*Echinacea purpurea*)
- Shasta Daisy (*Leucanthemum* hybrids)

Pinch late-flowering perennials back lightly to encourage bushier growth and more flowers.

Set up a feeder for ruby-throated hummingbirds. To make nectar, dissolve one part white sugar in four parts boiling water and let cool. Remember to clean your hummingbird feeder, all other feeders and birdbaths weekly by dipping them in a mild bleach solution, rinsing and refilling.

JUNE

*Timely weeding pays. Ten minutes
spent pulling tiny new weeds can prevent
an hour's worth of work later on when those
same weeds mature.*

*Keep soil moist around transplants
until they become established.*

*For a dense, smooth surface on pines,
shear the candles (new shoots) back by
one half to two thirds while still tender.
Thinning pruning creates a more natural
look and can be done anytime.*

Coreopsis (*left*) enlivens a summer garden with its
bright yellow, continuous blooms. Shear back
late summer for more flowers in fall. *Opposite
page, clockwise from top right:* abutilon trained
into a tree form; formal containers with vinca,
bacopa, verbena and other annuals; nasturtiums, daisies, geraniums, asparagus ferns
and bacopa in a terra-cotta pot.

CONTAINER GARDENING

Most plants can be grown in containers. Annuals, perennials, vegetables, shrubs and even trees can be adapted to container culture. There are many advantages to gardening in containers:

- They work well in small spaces. Even apartment dwellers with small balconies can enjoy the pleasures of gardening with planters on the balcony.
- They are mobile. Containers can be moved around to take advantage of light or shade and can even be moved into a sheltered location for winter.
- They are easier to reach. Container plantings allow people in wheelchairs or with back problems to garden without having to do a lot of bending.
- They are useful for extending the season. You can get an early start without the transplant shock that many plants suffer when moved outdoors. You can also protect plants from an early frost in fall.

JUNE

*Put trailing plants near the edge of
a container to spill out, and bushy and
upright plants in the middle where they will
give height and depth to the planting.*

*Consider mixing different plants together in
a container. You can create contrasts of
colour, texture and habit and give a small
garden an inviting appearance.*

*Mugo pine and dwarf Alberta spruce
are two winter-hardy evergreen shrubs that
will survive container life year-round.*

The flowers of *Salvia farinacea* 'Victoria' (*left*) are a
beautiful deep violet blue. They look stunning plante
with yellow or orange flowers such as nasturtiums,
coreopsis, California poppies or marigolds. *Opposite
page, clockwise from top left:* lettuce in a unique tu
planter; a deck improved by a vibrant container garde
terracotta pot filled with petunias, dahlias and ornamental millet; marigolds, sweet potato vine and beg
nias in planters

Gardeners can get over a month's head start on the gardening season by using containers. Tomatoes, pumpkins and watermelons can be started from seed in late April. Planted into large containers, they can be moved outside during warm days and brought back in at night as needed in April and May. This prevents the stretching that many early started plants suffer from if kept indoors for too long before being planted into the garden.

Many houseplants enjoy spending the summer outside in a shady location. The brighter a location you need to provide for your plant indoors, the better it will do outdoors. Avoid putting plants in direct sun because when you bring them back indoors at summer's end, they will have a hard time adjusting to the lower intensity of light.

JUNE

Keep an eye open for the early signs of pest and disease problems. They are easiest to deal with when they are just beginning.

Though considered old-fashioned or boring by some gardeners, petunias (*left*) are versatile and dependable annuals that bloom continuously in any sunny location. New varieties of this flower seem to appear every spring in Maritime garden centres. Spirea (*top right*) by water feature

Water gardens can be created in containers. Many ready-made container gardens are available, or you can create your own. Garden centres have lots of water garden supplies, and many water plants will grow as well in a large tub as they will in a pond.

Most perennials, shrubs or trees will require more winter protection in containers than they would if grown in the ground. Because the roots are above ground level, they are exposed to the winter wind and cycles of freezing and thawing. Protect container-grown plants by insulating the inside of the container. Thin sheets of foam insulation can be purchased and fitted around the inside of the pot before the soil is added. Containers can also be moved to sheltered locations. Garden sheds and unheated garages work well to protect plants from the cold and wind of winter.

A very natural look for informal ponds can be achieved by covering the rubber liner with beach rock and pebble (*right*). This also provides plenty of surface area for bacteria to colonize, which keep the water clear by consuming excess nutrients.

JULY

*The hot, sunny days of July encourage us
to sit back, relax and enjoy all the hard work
we've put into our gardens.*

JULY

1

2

Deadhead repeat-blooming annuals and perennials regularly to keep them looking their best.

3

4

Cut flowers to use in fresh arrangements indoors.

Faded green areas on dense evergreens in warm spots usually means spider mites are on the attack. Spraying the area with a mild dish soap and water solution should eliminate them.

5

6

7

The hardy shrub rose 'Bonica' (*left*) blooms profusely all summer, producing medium pink roses on a 1.2–1.5 m (4–5') wide bush. A riot of phlox, daylilies, yarrow, ageratum and snapdragons (*top right*); barberry (*bottom right*) tolerates dry conditions.

Flowerbeds have filled in; green tomatoes form on the vine. The season's transplants are established and need less frequent watering. By July, the days are long and warm. The garden appears to grow before your eyes. Some spring- blooming perennials become dormant while others thrive, filling in the spaces left by the earlier bloomers.

THINGS TO DO

Though droughts are uncommon in most of the Maritimes, rainfall can be irregular during July and August.

Water deeply, but no more than once a week during dry spells. Water early in the day to minimize potential disease and reduce water lost through evaporation.

Rocky ground and thin soil are two of the biggest complaints of Maritime gardeners. Mulch with compost to gradually boost your soil's organic content, water and nutrient retention.

Top up water gardens regularly if levels drop because of evaporation.

Thin vegetable crops such as beets, carrots and turnips. Crowded plants lead to poor crops.

Train new shoots of climbing vines such as morning glory and sweet peas to their supports.

JULY

8

9

Weed regularly to keep beds tidy.

10

11

Turn the compost pile, and when the compost is ready, add it to your flowerbeds and vegetable garden.

Fluff compacted mulch and cultivate bare soil areas to break the crust that forms in hot, dry weather. Doing so will allow air and water to get to plant roots.

12

13

14

Annual clary sage (*left*) loves sun, and its brilliantly coloured bracts attract butterflies and hummingbirds to the flowers. Plant it among other sun-loving annuals and perennials where its whites, pinks and purples will provide bright bursts of colour.
Opposite page, clockwise from top left: zinnias; statice; bachelor's buttons

❧

You can use an organic fertilizer on container plants and on garden plants if compost is scarce.

❧

Sawfly larvae may attack your spruce, pine, mountain ash and currant plants. To eliminate them easily, spray a solution of mild dish soap and water on affected areas.

❧

Pick zucchini when they are small. They are tender and tasty, and you are less likely to wind up with boxes full of foot-long zucchini to leave on unsuspecting neighbours' front doorsteps. Consider donating extra vegetables to a homeless shelter or food bank, where they will be much appreciated.

Plan to replace fading flowers and vegetables by sowing seeds for a fall display or crop. Peas, bush beans, annual candytuft and lobelia are often finished fruiting or blooming by mid- to late summer, leaving holes in the garden that can be filled by new plants. Seeds for replacement plants can be direct sown or started indoors.

JULY

15

16

Top mulch up if it is getting thin in places in your garden. Mulch protects roots, holds in moisture and helps keep weeds at bay.

17

18

Tie plants to their stakes as they grow.

Organic treatment for ant hills: loosen the soil and pour boiling water into them to avoid using toxic pesticides or gasoline.

19

20

Heliopsis (*left*), a native prairie perennial, is easy to grow and tolerates poor conditions, but it thrives in full sun and fertile, moist soil. Its name means 'resembling the sun' and its sunny blooms make long-lasting cut flowers. *Opposite page:* Use a mixture of annuals and perennials to decorate garden rooms (*top left*), escort visitors along a garden path (*top right*) or create a garden view (*bottom right*).

21

An important factor in ensuring the survival of a plant in your garden is where you plant it. Find out what the best growing conditions are for your new plant to thrive, and then plant it where these conditions exist in your yard. For example, a shrub that needs full sun will never do well in a north-facing location.

PLANT PROBLEMS

Problems such as chewed leaves, mildews and nutrient deficiencies tend to become noticeable in July when plants finish their first flush of growth and turn their attention to flowering and fruiting.

Such problems can be minimized if you develop a good problem-management program. Though it may seem complicated, problem management is a simple process that relies on correct and timely identification of the problem and then using the least environmentally harmful method to deal with it.

JULY

22

23

Trim or shear back early-flowering perennials when they have finished blooming.

24

25

Trim hedges regularly to keep them looking tidy and lush.

26

27

'Cupcake' (*left*) is a delightful miniature rose with a classic hybrid tea shape. It produces an abundance of blooms and is disease resistant. Like all hybrid roses, it needs special winter protection. *Opposite page, clockwise from top left:* deer-pruned white cedar; a swallowtail on cherry blossoms; a birdbath in a shade garden

28

Garden problems fall into three basic categories:

- pests, such as aphids, mites, caterpillars, mice and deer
- diseases, caused by bacteria, fungi and viruses
- physiological problems, caused by nutrient deficiencies, too much or too little water, incorrect light levels and severe exposure.

Choose healthy plants bred for disease and pest resistance and suited to the conditions of your garden.

Vegetable gardens may get raided by deer and raccoons. A safe, low-voltage electric fence is the best protection. Put wires at 15 cm (6"), 30 cm (12") and 102 cm (40"). See your farm supply dealer for advice and supplies.

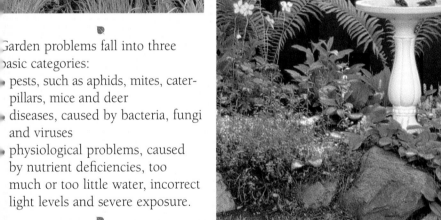

Prevention is the most important aspect of problem management. A healthy garden is resistant to problems and develops a natural balance between beneficial and detrimental organisms.

JULY

29

30

31

The natural pesticide pyrethrin is derived from certain species of chrysanthemums.

Annual cup-and-saucer vine (*below*) produces sweetly scented flowers that are cream coloured when they emerge and turn purple as they age. Ladybug (*top right*), a beneficial insect that feasts on aphids; Dahlberg daisies (*bottom right*)

PEST MANAGEMENT

Correct identification of problems is the key to solving them.
Just because an insect is on a
plant doesn't mean it's doing
any harm.

Chemical pest control should
always be the last alternative.
There are many alternatives
that pose no danger to gardeners or their families and pets.
• Cultural controls are the day-
  to-day gardening techniques
  you use to keep your garden
  healthy. Weeding, mulching,
  adding lots of organic matter
  to soil and growing problem-
  resistant cultivars are a few
  techniques you can use to
  keep gardens healthy.
• Physical controls are the
  hands-on part of problem
  solving. Picking insects off
  leaves, removing diseased
  foliage and creating barriers
  to stop rabbits from getting
  into the vegetable patch are
  examples of physical controls.
• Biological controls use natural
  and introduced populations
  of predators that prey on
  pests. Birds, snakes, frogs,
  spiders, some insects and
  even bacteria naturally feed
  on some problem insects. Soil
  microbes work with plant
  roots to increase their resistance to disease.

The pesticide industry has responded to
consumer demand for effective,
environmentally safe pest control
products. Natural pesticides are made
from plant, animal, bacterial or mineral
sources. They are effective in small
quantities and decompose quickly in the
environment. These products help reduce
our reliance on synthetic pesticides.

AUGUST

*Though the warm weather continues,
the ripening fruit, vegetables and seeds are
signs that summer is nearing its end.*

AUGUST

Reduce fertilizer applications to allow perennials, shrubs and trees ample time to harden off before the cold weather.

Continue to water during dry spells. Plants shouldn't need deep watering more than once a week at this time of the year.

Raccoons catching goldfish in ponds can be a problem. Ponds at least 2.4 m (8') wide by 61 cm (2') deep are resistant. Give fish a hiding place, such as a flagstone suspended on rocks high enough to swim under—they'll love it.

Calendula (*left*) is an easy flower to grow from seed. It blooms quickly in spring and all summer long, even tolerating light frost. It can be used as a culinary herb as well. *Opposite page, from top* geraniums; ripening apples; petunias

The warm days of July blend into August, but the nights are cooler and if it hasn't been too dry, many plants respond with a renewed display of colour.

THINGS TO DO

The garden seems to take care of itself in August. We gardeners putter about, tying up floppy hollyhock spikes, picking vegetables and pulling an odd weed, but the frenzy of early summer is over and we take the time just to sit and enjoy the results of our labours.

Continue to deadhead perennials and annuals to keep the blooms coming.

Remove worn-out annuals and vegetables, and replace them with new ones from the nursery or those you started last month. Shearing some annuals and perennials back will encourage new growth, giving them a fresh look for fall.

Keep an eye open for pests that may be planning to hibernate in the debris around your plants or the bark of your trees. Taking care of a few insects now may keep several generations out of your garden next summer.

Pick apples as soon as they are ready, being careful not to bruise the fruit.

AUGUST

Seed areas of the lawn that are thin or dead. Keep the seed well watered, if necessary, while it germinates.

Depending on the size of your perennials, you can divide them using a shovel or pitchfork (for large plants), a sharp knife (for small plants) or your hands (for easily divided plants).

A few drops of mineral oil on new corn silk safely discourages corn earworm.

The French marigold (*left*) is just one variety of this popular annual. All marigolds are low-maintenance plants that stand up well to heat, wind and rain.

PLANT PROPAGATION

Now is a good time to divide some perennials and to note which of your plants will need dividing next spring. Look for these signs that perennials need dividing:

- The centre of the plant has died.
- The plant is not flowering as profusely as it did in previous years.
- The plant is encroaching on the growing space of others.

August is a good time to propagate plants. Taking cuttings and gathering seed are great ways to increase your plant collection and to share some of your favourite plants with friends and family.

Plants such as Siberian bugloss (*top left*), anemone (*top right*), evening primrose (*centre*) and liatris (*right*) are good plants to divide if you're just starting your perennial collection. They recover and fill in quickly when divided.

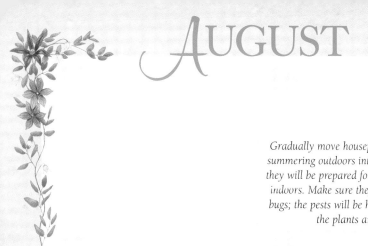

AUGUST

Gradually move houseplants that have been summering outdoors into shadier locations so they will be prepared for the lower light levels indoors. Make sure they aren't infested with bugs; the pests will be harder to control once the plants are indoors.

Turn the layers of the compost pile and continue to add garden soil, kitchen scraps and garden debris that isn't diseased or infested with insects.

Remove the top 10 cm (4") or so from Brussel sprouts stems to force larger heads to develop

Verbena (*left*) works well in full sun and can be used as a groundcover, in beds, along borders or in containers. *Opposite page, clockwise from top left:* basket-of-gold, sedum and aster are easy to propagate from stem cuttings.

Perennials, trees, shrubs and tender perennials that are treated as annuals can all be started from cuttings. This method is an excellent way to propagate varieties and cultivars that you really like but that are slow or difficult to start from seed or that don't produce viable seed.

There is some debate over what size cuttings should be. Some claim that smaller cuttings are more likely to root and will root more quickly. Others claim that larger cuttings develop more roots and become established more quickly once planted. Try different sizes and see what works best for you.

The easiest cuttings to take from woody plants such as trees, shrubs and vines are called semi-ripe, semi-mature or semi-hardwood cuttings. They are taken from mature new growth that has not yet become completely woody, usually in late summer or early fall.

AUGUST

Continue watering newly planted perennials, trees and shrubs if dry weather occurs. Water deeply to encourage root growth

Avoid pruning rust-prone plants such as mountain ash and crabapple in late summer and fall because many rusts are releasing spores now.

A quick, effective, organic method to eliminate sidewalk weeds is to pour scalding water on them.

You won't need to collect seed from borage (*left*) because these plants self-seed profusely and will no doubt turn up in your garden next spring. *Opposite page, clockwise from top left:* larkspur; nasturtiums with creeping Jenny; zinnias

You'll save money over the years by collecting seeds of annual plants. Choose plants that are not hybrids or the seeds will probably not come true to type and may not germinate at all. A few plants easy to collect from are listed below:

- Borage (*Borago officinalis*)
- Calendula (*Calendula officinalis*)
- Coriander (*Coriandrum sativum*)
- Dill (*Anethum graveolens*)
- Fennel (*Foeniculum vulgare*)
- Larkspur (*Consolida ajacis*)
- Marigold (*Tagetes* spp.)
- Nasturtium (*Tropaeolum majus*)
- Poppy (*Papaver rhoeas*)
- Zinnia (*Zinnia elegans*)

Always make cuttings just below a leaf node, the point where the leaves are attached to the stem.

Many gardeners enjoy the hobby of collecting and planting seed. You need to know a few basic things before you begin:

- Know your plant. Correctly identify the plant and learn about its life cycle. You will need to know when it flowers, when the seeds are likely to ripen and how the plant disperses its seeds in order to collect them.
- Find out if there are special requirements for starting the seeds. For example, do they need a hot or cold period to germinate?

AUGUST

Find a source of straw for mulching and decorating now because it can be harder to find later in fall.

Nasturtiums (*below*) are versatile annuals. Their edibl
flowers and foliage are attractive additions to baskets and containers as well as to salads. Even the
seedpods can be pickled and used as a substitute
for capers. *Opposite page, clockwise from top left:*
golden clematis flowers and seedheads; Oriental
poppy; Hens and Chickens poppy seedpod

When collecting seeds, consider the following:

- Collect seeds once they are ripe but before they are shed from the parent plant.
- Remove capsules, heads or pods as they begin to dry and remove the seeds later, once they are completely dry.
- Place a paper bag over a seed-head as it matures and loosely tie it in place to collect seeds as they are shed.
- Dry seeds after they've been collected. Place them on a paper-lined tray and leave them in a warm, dry location for one to three weeks.
- Separate seeds from the other plant parts before storing.
- Store seeds in air-tight containers in a cool, frost-free location.

Don't collect seeds or plants from the wild because harvesting from natural areas is severely depleting many plant populations. Many species and populations of wild plants are protected, and it is illegal to collect their seeds.

Collecting and saving seeds is a time-honoured tradition. Early settlers brought seeds with them when they came to North America and saved them carefully each fall for the following spring.

SEPTEMBER

Though we cling tenaciously to any summer weather that lingers, there's no denying that fall is upon us.

SEPTEMBER

1

2

Time to stop fertilizing, but consider topdressing your garden with compost. Start gathering your leaves and garden waste from this season to make new compost.

3

4

Plant colourful fall ornamentals, such as chrysanthemums, flowering cabbage and flowering kale, available in fall at most garden centres

5

6

Weak, declining flowering crab, mountain ash or apple trees may have borers in the trunk at ground level. Look for small holes and 'sawdust.' Squirt an organic remedy into holes because borers kill young trees.

7

Goldenrod (*left*), amaranthus (*top right*), strawflower (*centre right*) and nigella (*bottom right*) can be harvested now for dried flower arrangements.

L eaves begin to change colour, seedheads nod in the breeze and brightly coloured berries and fruit adorn many trees and shrubs. There is a slight chance of frost in some gardens before the end of September, but on a warm afternoon summer can seem endless. Many annuals are undamaged by early frosts and continue to bloom until the first hard freeze.

THINGS TO DO

Having enjoyed another summer garden, your big fall clean up begins.

Take advantage of end-of-season sales. Many garden centres are getting rid of trees, shrubs and perennials at reduced prices. There is still plenty of time for the roots to become established before the ground freezes. Do not buy plants that are excessively root bound.

Consider starting some herb seeds now. You can plant them in pots and keep them in a bright window so you'll have fresh herbs to add to soups and salads over winter. Moving herb plants in from outdoors is also possible, but the plants often have a difficult time adapting to the lower light levels indoors.

SEPTEMBER

8

9

Dig up tuberous tender plants such as begonias for drying and storing over winter before the first frost. Wait to dig up dahlias until the first frost hits the leaves.

10

11

Though the garden may be getting lots of rain now, make sure to water beds under the overhangs of the house. Soil must be kept moist right up to hard freeze.

12

13

14

Lilies are long-lived, easy-to-grow perennials. They look superb in floral arrangements combined with flowers such as baby's breath (*left*). *Opposite page, clockwise from top left:* the fall colours and features of Virginia creeper, burning bush, full moon maple and ginkgo

If you've let your weeds get out of hand over summer, be sure to pull them up before they set seed to avoid having even more weeds popping up in the garden next summer.

Cool fall weather is ideal for sowing grass seed and repairing thin patches in the lawn. Get seeding done by October 1.

The changing colours are a sure sign that fall is here. Bright reds, golds, bronzes and coppers seem to give warmth to a cool day. The display doesn't have to be reserved for a walk in the park. Include trees and shrubs with good fall colour, such as the ones listed here, in your garden:

- Maple (*Acer*)
- Burning Bush (*Euonymus alatus*)
- Boston Ivy (*Parthenocissus tricuspidata*)
- Cotoneaster (*Cotoneaster*)
- Witch-hazel (*Hamamelis*)

SEPTEMBER

15

16

Set up birdfeeders and begin to feed the birds if you didn't do so all summer.

17

Move tender container plants into a sheltered location or cover with a sheet when frost is expected. This strategy will allow you to enjoy them for longer.

18

To grow oak or horse chestnut, plant newly fallen nuts 3" deep in a garden bed along the house, water and mulch them over. They survive winter best in a sheltered spot.

19

20

The cheery golden marguerite daisy (*below*) forms a tidy mound that works wonderfully in both formal and informal garden settings. *Opposite page, clockwise from top left:* Asiatic lily 'Electra'; fancy tulips; black-eyed Susan; alliums

21

Begin to plant bulbs for a great display next spring. Tulips, daffodils, crocuses, scillas, muscaris and alliums are just a few of the bulbs whose flowers will welcome you back into the garden next year.

Spring-flowering perennials such as primroses and candytuft will be a delightful sight come April and May and can be planted now.

For vivacious colour from summer through fall, a continuously blooming perennial such as black-eyed Susan can't be beat.

SEPTEMBER

22

23

When planting bulbs, you may want to add a little bonemeal to the soil to encourage root development.

24

25

Check houseplants for insect pests before moving them back indoors for winter.

Press fall leaves at their peak in layers of newsprint for dried arrangements all winter.

26

27

28

Echinacea purpurea (left), commonly called purple coneflower and used as a popular herbal cold remedy, is a long-blooming, drought-resistant perennial. Its distinctively cone-shaped flowers look good in fresh and dried floral arrangements. *Opposite page:* Ponds, fruiting trees and tall flowering perennials such as bee balm, coneflower and yarrow attract wildlife to your yard.

CREATING WILDLIFE HABITAT

The rapid rate of urban sprawl has led to the relentless expansion of large cities and a loss of habitat for wildlife. Our gardens can easily restore some of the space, shelter, food and water that wildlife needs. Here are a few tips for attracting wildlife to your garden:

- Make sure at least some of the plants in your garden are locally native. Birds and small animals are used to eating native plants, so they'll visit a garden that has them. When selecting non-native plants for your yard, choose those that wildlife might also find appealing, such as shrubs that bear fruit.
- Provide a source of water. A pond with a shallow side or a birdbath will offer water for drinking and bathing. Frogs and toads eat a wide variety of insect pests and will happily take up residence in or near a ground-level water feature.

Many Maritime backyards border woodland. Dispose of your brush in small piles just out of sight to provide wildlife with shelter as the piles slowly rot away.

- A variety of birdfeeders and seed will encourage different species of birds to visit your garden. Some birds will visit an elevated feeder, but others prefer a feeder set at or near ground level. Fill your feeders regularly but especially when birds' natural food supplies may be low (e.g., winter, early spring). They will appreciate an extra, reliable food source.

SEPTEMBER

29

30

*Pull out annual plants and vegetables
as they fade or are killed by frost.*

Zinnias (*below*) are easy annuals to grow, come in a
rainbow of colours and make long-lasting cut flowers for floral arrangements. *Opposite page, clockwise from top left:* birdfeeder; monarda with butterfly; sunflower; maple tree

- Butterflies, hummingbirds and a wide variety of predatory insects will be attracted if you include lots of pollen-producing plants in your garden. Plants such as golden-rod, comfrey, bee balm, salvia, Joe-Pye weed, black-eyed Susan, catmint, purple coneflower, coreopsis, hollyhock and yarrow will attract pollen lovers.

- Shelter is the final aspect to keeping your resident wildlife happy. Patches of dense shrubs, tall grasses and mature trees provide shelter. As well, you can leave a small pile of twiggy brush in an out-of-the-way place. Nature stores and many garden centres sell toad houses and birdhouses.

Inevitably squirrels and chipmunks will try to get at your birdfeeders. Instead of trying to get rid of them, why not leave peanuts and seeds out for them as well? Place them near a tree, where they can easily get at them. If you have a large spruce tree, they will eat the seeds out of the cones. Leave cones out with the other food offerings. The little cone scales that are left when they are done can be composted for the garden or used to prevent slipping on icy walks and driveways.

OCTOBER

This month marks the inevitable end of summer. Frosts and falling leaves remind us that winter is not far off.

OCTOBER

Try to get bulbs planted by mid month so they can grow their new roots this fall for good spring performance.

Lawn mowing comes to an end soon. Leave the grass neat but not too short for the winter.

Last chance to divide and plant perennials that need 4–6 weeks to settle in before winter begins.

Collect newly fallen Austrian, Scots and white pine cones to dry for Christmas decorating.

If the first frost hasn't yet arrived and your apples are still on the tree (*left*), now is the time to harvest them. However, some varieties taste better after the first frost. *Opposite page, clock-wise from top:* colourful fall foliage; a bountiful harvest of carrots; endearing teddy bear sunflower

The garden may still be vigorous early in the month, but by Halloween, only the hardy bloomers may still be going strong. Though we may wake up some mornings to a frost-dusted world, it is more likey that we will be enduring the inevitable wet weather. Enjoy any warm weather. Jumping into raked up piles of leaves is a pleasure that need not be reserved for the young.

THINGS TO DO

October is the time to finish tidying up and putting the garden to bed for another year.

Harvest any remaining vegetables. Soft fruit such as tomatoes and zucchini should be harvested before the first frost, but cool weather vegetables such as carrots, cabbage, Brussels sprouts and turnips can wait a while longer because they are frost hardy.

Unless your plants have been afflicted with some sort of disease, you can leave faded perennial growth in place and clean it up in spring. The stems will collect leaves and snow, protecting the roots and crown of the plant over the winter.

OCTOBER

Continue to tidy up dead plant material. Most can be composted, but diseased material is better thrown out.

Start mulching the garden, but avoid covering plants completely until the ground has frozen. Doing so prevents plants from rotting and deters small rodents from digging down and feasting on plant roots and crowns.

Collect and freeze berry-laden mountain ash and cranberry branch tips to feed the birds all winter.

The serviceberry (*left*) is a small tree that bears whit͏e flowers in spring, edible red berries in summer and lovely orange-red foliage in fall. It requires little maintenance and does quite well near water.

Fall is a great time to improve your soil. Amendments added now can be worked in lightly. By planting time next spring, the amendments will have been further worked in by the actions of worms and soil microorganisms and by the freezing and thawing that takes place over winter.

Local farmers' markets are often the best places to find a wide variety of seasonal vegetables and flowers (*above and below*).

Things to do with your fall leaves: add them to the compost pile; gather them into their own compost pile to decompose into leaf mold; rototill them into your vegetable garden; or mow them over and then pile them onto flowerbeds. Whole leaves can become matted together, encouraging fungal disease.

Don't let your goldfish pond freeze solid with ice. Remove the larger falls pump, and place a small pump on the bottom of the pond aimed upwards to keep an open spot for gases to escape all winter. Check the hole periodically to ensure it stays open.

OCTOBER

Continue to water trees and shrubs
until the ground freezes up. Apply an organic
anti-desiccant to newly planted evergreens
to reduce winter moisture loss.

Faded annuals and vegetables can be
pulled up and added to the compost pile.

Poppy seedheads make great eyes
for your jack 'o lantern.

Honeysuckle vine (*left*) flowers from summer to fall
frost. Prune in spring to cut back dead growth as new
leaves emerge. Composting (*far right*); delicious fruit
and vegetables harvested from the garden (*near right*)

COMPOSTING

One of the best additives for any type of soil is compost. Compost can be purchased at most garden centres, and many communities now have composting programs. You can easily make compost in your own garden. Though garden refuse and vegetable scraps from your kitchen left in a pile will eventually decompose, it is possible to produce compost more quickly. Here are a few suggestions for creating compost:

- Compost decomposes most quickly when there is a balance between brown and green materials. There should be more brown matter, such as chopped straw or shredded leaves, than green matter, such as vegetable scraps and grass clippings.
- Layer the brown and the green matter, and mix in some garden soil or previously finished compost. This step introduces decomposer organisms to the pile.

OCTOBER

As outdoor gardening winds down, try starting bulbs such as paperwhites (narcissus) indoors. Fragrant white blooms should emerge in a few weeks.

Cure pumpkins and winter squash (acorn, buttercup, hubbard, etc.) in a cool, frost-free location before storing for winter.

Fertilize deciduous trees and shrubs after leaf drop.

Yarrow's showy, flat-topped flower-heads (*left*) provide months of continuous colour in summer, and the seedheads persist into winter.

Compost won't decompose properly if it is too wet or too dry. Keep the pile covered during heavy rain and sprinkle it with water if it is too dry. The correct level of moisture can best be described as that of a wrung-out sponge.

To aerate the pile, use a garden fork to poke holes in it or turn it regularly. Use a thermometer with a long probe attached, similar to a large meat thermometer, to check the temperature in your pile. When the temperature reaches 70° C (158° F), give the pile a turn.

Finished compost is dark in color and light in texture. When you can no longer recognize what went into the compost, it is ready for use.

Compost can be mixed into garden soil or spread on the surface as a mulch.

Images of fall: ripe pumpkins (*top left*); juicy clusters of vine-ripened grapes (*top right*); tasty corn on the cob fresh from the garden (*above*). Many gardeners find fruiting plants to be decorative as well as useful.

OCTOBER

If you don't have the time or the inclination to fuss over your compost, you can just leave it in a pile and it will eventually decompose with no added assistance from you.

Sunflowers (*below*) are synonymous with fall for many gardeners. Their bold yellow, seed-filled flowerheads celebrate the harvest season and provide treats for the birds. Canada serviceberry (*top right*) and viburnum (*centre right*) both bear berries in fall. The fruit attracts birds and can be used to make jellies, pies and wine.

Before adding specific nutrients to your soil, you should get a soil test done. Simple kits to test for pH and major nutrients are available at garden centres. More thorough tests can be done; consult your provincial agriculture department for information. These tests will tell you what the pH is, the comparative levels of sand, silt, clay and organic matter and the quantities of all required nutrients. They will also tell you what amendments to add and in what quantities to improve your soil.

Adding amendments to your soil will alter its condition, depending on what's required:
- Compost can be mixed into a clay soil to loosen the structure and allow water to penetrate.
- Elemental sulfur, peat moss or pine needles added on a regular basis can make soil under rhododendrons more acidic.
- Calcitic or dolomitic limestone, hydrated lime, quicklime or wood ashes can be added to an acidic soil to make it more alkaline.

Sunflowers (*above*) and other cut flowers can be found in abundance in farmers' markets. Use them for fresh or dried table arrangements, or flower pressing for winter crafts.

NOVEMBER

Branches lie bare, dry flowerheads sway in the breeze and excited birds pick brightly colored fruit from frost-covered branches.

NOVEMBER

After raking and once the lawn is dormant, apply an organic fertilizer. If you haven't needed to mow in a couple of weeks, it is probably sufficiently dormant.

If you have healthy willows, dogwoods, Virginia creeper or evergreens, cut a few branches to use in Christmas wreaths. Store in a cool place until needed.

Thinning pruning of shrubs can continue up until hard freeze. There's more time now than during the spring rush.

Compact, bushy and cold-hardy to zone 2b, the Champlain Explorer (*left*) produces abundant clusters of velvety red roses almost all summer long and is resistant to black spot and powdery mildew.

Despite the inevitable frosts, a few stragglers always hang on. Flowers like pansies keep blooming, even under a light blanket of snow, until the ground starts to freeze. A fall of wet snow draws children into the garden, happy to build a snowman on the lawn.

THINGS TO DO

Garden tasks this month involve tucking the garden in for winter.

Harvest any remaining vegetables. Root vegetables, such as carrots, parsnips and turnips, and green vegetables, such as cabbages and broccoli, store well in a cool place, and their flavour is often improved after a touch of frost.

The garden can be quite beautiful in November, especially when persistent fruit becomes more visible on branches (*below*), after a light dusting of snow or frost (*right*) or dripping with rain.

NOVEMBER

8   9

Clear away tools, hoses and garden furniture
before the snow flies so they won't be
damaged by the cold and wet weather.

10   11

Mound mulch around the bases of semi-
hardy shrubs once the ground freezes
to protect the roots and stem bases
from temperature fluctuations.

12   13

To leave your potentillas and spireas neat
and set for spring growth, shear them
to about half their size, then thin out
8–10 older stems to the ground.

14

The beautiful hybrid tea rose 'Rosemary
Harkness' (*left*) produces fragrant orange
yellow double blooms from summer t
autumn. Like other tender hybrid te
it should be protected from any
harsh winter weather. The richly
coloured rosettes of ornamental ka
(*top right*) are reminiscent of roses
(*top left*); strawberry (*centre right*);
coastal woodland (*bottom right*)

Prepare hybrid tea and other semi-hardy roses for winter before the ground freezes. Mound dirt up over the base and cover with mulch, or surround the plant with loose, quick-drying material, such as sawdust, shredded leaves or peat moss, and cover with a wooden box. Hold the box in place with a heavy rock on top when you are done.

Avoid completely covering perennials with mulch until the ground freezes. Mound the mulch around them (*above*) and store some extra mulch in a frost-free location to add once they are frozen. If you pile the mulch in the garden, you may find it has also frozen solid when you want to use it.

NOVEMBER

Be sure to enjoy any remaining warm days before the garden becomes the dream of next summer.

Fill your birdfeeders regularly. Well-fed birds will continue to visit your garden in summer, feeding on undesirable insects in your garden.

Clean tools thoroughly and wipe them with an oily rag to prevent them from rusting. Sharpen pruners, shovels and spades before storing them for winter.

Pieris (left); opposite page, clockwise from top left: mountain ash, staghorn sumac, nest spruce and serviceberry

our garden doesn't have to be right on the coast to experience some of the same conditions. The wind can carry the salty air inland far from the coast. If this is a problem in some or all of your garden, consider growing salt and seaside-tolerant plants such as Austrian pine, mountain ash, nest spruce, serviceberry, sumac, thyme, creeping juniper, pinks, common thrift, nasturtiums and geraniums. A walk in a local wilderness area or park can give you lots of ideas for what to include in your own garden.

Now that you've had the chance to observe your garden for a growing season, consider the microclimates and think about how you can put them to good use. Are any always quick to dry? Do some areas stay wet longer than others? What area is the most sheltered? Which is the least sheltered? Cater your plantings to the microclimates of your garden.

NOVEMBER

Large, heavy perennial clumps can still be moved, but smaller pieces are prone to frost heave and winter kill.

Anti-dessicant spray can be applied now to newer evergreens in exposed sites to limit the drying that causes winter burn.

To deter deer from eating your evergreens, plant species they don't prefer: pine, spruce, juniper, false cypress and rhododendron. Avoid their favourites—yew, eunonymous and cedar.

Flowers such as marsh marigolds (*left*), irises (*top left and right*), daylilies (*centre right*) and ligularia (*bottom right*) work well in damp areas of the garden because they prefer moist growing conditions.

BOG GARDENING

Turn a damp area into your own little bog garden. Dig out a damp area 35–50 cm (14–20") below ground level, line with a piece of punctured pond liner and fill with soil. The area will stay wet but still allow some water to drain away, providing a perfect location to plant moisture-loving perennials. A few to consider are,

- Astilbe (*Astilbe* spp. and hybrids)
- Cardinal Flower (*Lobelia* x *speciosa*)
- Daylily (*Hemerocallis* hybrids)
- Doronicum (*Doronicum orientale*)
- Goat's beard (*Aruncus dioicus*)
- Hosta (*Hosta* hybrids)
- Iris (*Iris ensata, I. siberica*)
- Ligularia (*Ligularia dentata*)
- Marsh Marigold (*Caltha palustris*)
- Meadowsweet (*Filipendula rubra* and *ulmaria*)
- Primrose (*Primula japonica*)
- Rodgersia (*Rodgersia aesculifolia* and *pinnata*)

NOVEMBER

Finish collecting seeds from open-pollinated flowers and vegetables. Stored in a cool, dry place, they will be ready for planting in next year's garden.

Japanese maple (*top left*); bigleaf hydrangea (*top right*); magnolia (*centre right*); Kousa dogwood (*bottom right*)

Rodgersia (*left*) bears bold foliage and fluffy flower plumes in mid- to late summer. It does best in a site sheltered from strong winds and extreme weather. Rodgersia plants prefer moist soil.

It is possible to grow out-of-zone plants. Reserve the warmest, most sheltered area of the garden for plants not considered fully hardy. Big leaf hydrangea, Japanese maple, magnolia and exotic dogwoods may survive in sheltered locations.

If you have a very exposed area in your garden, you can find plants that will do well there, or you can make a planting that will shelter the area. A hedge or group of trees or shrubs will break the wind and provide an attractive feature for your garden.

DECEMBER

Already summer seems far away. Ghostly forms and dashes of colour are all that remain to inspire us until spring.

DECEMBER

1

2

Light levels are low, so cycle your houseplants from darker to lighter rooms to give each some time by the brightest windows to stay healthy.

3

4

Maritime gardeners can have beautiful holly like that seen in warmer climates. Blue holly (Ilex x meserveae) thrives in sheltered beds, reaching 1.5–2.4 m (5–8') in diameter. Thin-prune it in early December for Christmas decorating.

5

6

A little wood ash added to your vegetable garden will help, but not too much. Any extra makes a good traction aid for icy driveways.

7

Holly ('Blue Girl' blue holly, *left*) makes an attractive addition to fresh winter arrangements. To keep it looking its best, keep the cut ends consistently moist. *Opposite page, clockwise from top left:* seasonal centrepiece; Swiss stone pine provides year round interest; decorative Christmas peppers are ideal for holiday colour indoors

Seasonal centerpiece (*left*) made with evergreen clippings from the yard: white pine, blue spruce, hemlock, cedar, yew, blue holly, balsam fir and false cypress.

The garden begins its winter display of colourful and peeling bark, branches with persistent fruit and evergreen boughs. With a bit of luck, snow begins to pile up on garden beds, covering withered perennials and shrubs and clinging to evergreen branches. Winter arrives, hopefully in time for the holidays, leaving only our fond memories of the garden.

THINGS TO DO

Our thoughts turn to indoor gardening though we may still have a few garden tasks to complete before we call it a year.

If rabbits and mice are a problem in your garden, you can protect your trees and shrubs with chicken wire. Wrap it around the plant bases and higher up the tree or shrub than you expect the snow to reach.

Gently brush snow off flexible evergreen branches. Heavy snow can weigh down juniper and white cedar branches enough to permanently bend them.

Check the soil in the beds under the overhangs. Watering to get soil moist before freeze up will keep the plants healthy.

DECEMBER

8

9

Move clay and concrete pots and statues into a protected location to prevent them from cracking over winter.

10

11

Reduce watering and cease feeding houseplants.

12

13

Rooting slips of houseplants often works as well in moist potting soil as it does in water, and it eliminates one step.

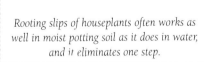

14

Poinsettias (*left*) add rich colour and beauty to our homes during the dark days of December. *Opposite page, clockwise from top left:* bonsai; *Cattleya* orchid; *Miltonopsis* orchid; spider plant

HOUSEPLANT CARE

You don't have to forget gardening completely when the snow begins to fly. All you have to do is turn your attention to indoor gardening. Houseplants clean the air, soften the hard edges of a room and provide colour, texture and interest to your home.

Just as you did for the garden outdoors, match your indoor plants to the conditions your home provides. If a room receives little light, try houseplants that require very low light levels. Plants that like humid conditions may do best in your bathroom where showering and the toilet bowl full of water maintain higher moisture levels than in any other room. Low-light-tolerant plants include philodendron, spider plant, cast iron plant and snake plant; bright-light-tolerant plants include cacti, jade plant and goldfish plant.

15

16

Most indoor plant pests can be controlled
by wiping leaves with a damp sponge.
More difficult pests can be controlled
with insecticidal soap.

17

18

Any herbs you are growing indoors
should be kept in the brightest window
you have to prevent them from becoming
too straggly or dying.

19

20

Although orchids are reputed to be difficult and
needy, the moth orchid *Phalaenopsis* (*left*) is easy to
grow on a windowsill. There are many thousands of
species of orchids in an amazing array of sizes, shapes,
colours and fragrances. Pearl plant and tiger jaws
(*centre right*); Japanese sago palm (*bottom right*)

21

There are three aspects of interior light to consider: intensity, duration and quality. Intensity is the difference between a south window with full sun and a north window with no direct sunlight. Duration is how long the light lasts in a specific location. An east window will have a shorter duration of light than a south window. Quality refers to the spectrum of the light. Natural light provides a broader spectrum than artificial light.

Watering is a key element to houseplant care. Overwatering can be as much of a problem as under watering. As you did with your garden plants, water thoroughly and infrequently. Let the soil dry out a bit before watering. Some plants are the exception to this rule. Find out what the water requirements of your houseplants are so you will have an idea of how frequently or infrequently you will need to water.

Look for creative ways to display your plants and add beauty to your home. Indoor fountains and moisture-loving plants, such as a peace lily in a vase of water (*top*), are interesting and attractive to look at. They add a decorative touch to a houseplant display.

22

23

Dust on plants is more than just an eyesore. It prevents plants from making full use of the light they receive. Clean leaves regularly with a damp cloth or sponge, or place them in the shower and let the water stream wash away any dust.

24

25

Poinsettias last longest when kept in a cool bright room with moist soil that isn't allowed to dry out completely.

26

27

Twigs from your garden make an excellent, natural-looking climbing structure for potted vines.

28

English ivy (*left*) that you've grown outdoors all summer can be brought indoors and kept as a houseplant in winter. Succulent and cacti display (*top right*); snake plant (*bottom right*), a striking, long-lived indoor plant

Houseplants generally only need fertilizer when they are actively growing. Always use a weak fertilizer to avoid burning the roots. Never feed plants when they are very dry. Moisten the soil by watering and then feed a couple of days later.

When repotting, go up by only one size at a time. In general the new pot should be no more than 5–10 cm (2–4") larger in diameter than the previous pot. If you find your soil drying out too frequently, then you may wish to use a larger pot that will stay moist for longer.

Houseplants are more than just attractive—they clean the air in our homes. Many dangerous and common toxins, such as benzene, formaldehyde and trichloroethylene are absorbed and eliminated by houseplants.

Here are a few easy-to-grow, toxin-absorbing houseplants:

- Bamboo Palm (*Chamaedorea erumpens*)
- Chinese Evergreen (*Aglaonema modestum*)
- Dragon Tree (*Dracaena marginata*)
- English Ivy (*Hedera helix*)
- Gerbera Daisy (*Gerbera jamesonii*)
- Peace Lily (*Spathiphyllum* 'Mauna Loa')
- Pot Mum (*Chrysanthemum morifolium*)
- Snake Plant (*Sansevieria trifasciata*)
- Spider Plant (*Chlorophytum comosum*)
- Weeping Fig (*Ficus benjamina*)

DECEMBER

29

30

Plants can be grouped together in large containers to more easily meet the needs of the plants. Cacti can be planted together in a gritty soil mix and placed in a dry, bright location. Moisture- and humidity-loving plants can be planted in a large terrarium where moisture levels remain higher.

31

A bouquet of cheerful gerberas and painted daisies (*below*) will brighten a drab winter day and remind you of summer, when these flowers were growing in your garden. Fiddle-leaf fig, tricolor dracaena and snake plant (*top left*); burro's tail (*top right*)

Keep in mind that many common houseplants dislike the dry winter air in our homes. Most will thrive in cooler, moister conditions than the typical home provides. Always turn thermostats down at night and create moist conditions by sitting pots on pebble trays. Water in the pebble tray can evaporate but won't soak excessively into the soil of the pot because the pebbles hold it above the water.

There's nothing like treating yourself to a bouquet of fresh flowers (*above*) when you're feeling the doldrums of winter. Many beautiful varieties are available. Watch for some of the more exotic plants from South America and Australia at grocery stores and florist shops.

RESOURCES

All resources cited were accurate at the time of publication. Please note that addresses, phone numbers and web sites/emails may change over time.

BOOKS

Armitage, Allan M. 2000. *Armitage's Garden Perennials*. Timber Press, Portland, OR.

Brickell, C., T.J. Cole and J.D. Zuk, eds. 1996. *Reader's Digest A–Z Encyclopedia of Garden Plants*. The Reader's Digest Association Ltd., Montreal, PQ.

Brickell, Christopher and David Joyce. 1996. *Eyewitness Garden Handbook: Pruning and Training*. Dorling Kindersley, London, England.

Bubel, Nancy. 1988. *The New Seed Starter's Handbook*. Rodale Press, Emmaus, PA.

Burrows, Roger. 2002. *Birds of Atlantic Canada*. Lone Pine Publishing, Edmonton, AB.

Courtier, Jane and Graham Clarke. 1997. *Indoor Plants: The Essential Guide to Choosing and Caring for Houseplants*. Reader's Digest, Westmount, PQ.

Dirr, Michael A. 1997. *Dirr's Hardy Trees and Shrubs*. Timber Press, Portland, OR.

Ellis, B.W. and F.M. Bradley, eds. 1996. *The Organic Gardener's Handbook of Natural Insect and Disease Control*. Rodale Press, Emmaus, PA.

Gilman, Edward F. 2002. *An Illustrated Guide to Pruning*. Delmar Publishing, Albany, NY.

Heintzelman, Donald S. 2001. *The Complete Backyard Birdwatcher's Home Companion*. Ragged Mountain Press, Camden, ME.

Hole, Lois. 1993. *Lois Hole's Vegetable Favorites*. Lone Pine Publishing, Edmonton, AB.

——. 1994. *Lois Hole's Bedding Plant Favorites*. Lone Pine Publishing, Edmonton, AB.

——. 1995. *Lois Hole's Perennial Favorites*. Lone Pine Publishing, Edmonton, AB.

——. 1996. *Lois Hole's Tomato Favorites*. Lone Pine Publishing, Edmonton, AB.

——. 1997. *Lois Hole's Rose Favorites*. Lone Pine Publishing, Edmonton, AB.

——. 1997. *Lois Hole's Favorite Trees and Shrubs*. Lone Pine Publishing, Edmonton, AB.

Hill, Lewis. 1991. *Secrets of Plant Propagation*. Storey Communications Inc., Pownal, VT.

Johnson, Lorraine. 1999. *100 Easy-to-Grow Native Plants for Canadian Gardens*. Random House of Canada/Denise Schon Books Inc., Toronto, ON.

Laird, Arlette. 2000. *The Joy of Planting: 101 Recipes for Pots and Containers*. Piroutte Publications, Prince Albert, SK.

McHoy, Peter. 2002. *Houseplants*. Hermes House, New York, NY.

McVicar, Jekka. 1997. *Jekka's Complete Herb Book*. Raincoast Books, Vancouver, BC.

Merilees, Bill. 1989. *Attracting Backyard Wildlife: A Guide for Nature Lovers*. Voyageur Press, Stillwater, MN.

Robinson, Peter. 1997. *Complete Guide to Water Gardening*. Reader's Digest, Westmount, PQ.

Thompson, P. 1992. *Creative Propagation: A Grower's Guide*. Timber Press, Portland, OR.

ONLINE RESOURCES

Aquatics & Co. Comprehensive water gardening information and products.
www.aquaticsco.com

Attracting Wildlife to your yard.com. How to make your backyard inviting to compatible and beneficial creatures.
www.attracting-wildlife-to-your-garden.com

Backyard Gardener. Gardening information, a newsletter, articles and online shopping.
www.backyardgardener.com

Butterfly Website. Learn about the fascinating world of butterflies.
www.butterflywebsite.com

Canadian Gardening. Ask the expert section and an extensive listing of gardening catalogues.
www.canadiangardening.com/home.html

Canadian Organic Growers. Fantastic information on organic growing.
www.cog.ca

Canadian Wildlife Federation. Everything you wanted to know about attracting wildlife.
www.cwf-fcf.org/

Composting Council of Canada. A national nonprofit organization that encourages composting.
www.compost.org

Evergreen Foundation. Tools to transform residential and commercial spaces into healthy outdoor spaces.
www.evergreen.ca/en/index.html

Halifax Seed. Canada's oldest mail order seed company.
http://shop.timwebworks.com/halifaxseed/

I Can Garden. Information and a gardening forum where you can contact gardeners from across Canada and the world.
www.icangarden.com/

North American Native Plant Society. Dedicated to the study, conservation and restoration of native plants.
www.nanps.org/index.shtml

Nova Scotia Department of Agriculture and Fisheries. Information on organic gardening for the home gardener.
http://www.gov.ns.ca/nsaf/elibrary/archive/hort/organic/pihor96-03.htm

Nova Scotia Organic Growers Association. A grassroots movement promoting wholesome food, sustainable communities and wise stewardship of the earth.
http://gks.com/NSOGA/

Nova Scotia Plant Savers. Dedicated to protecting native medicinal plants of Canada and the US and promoting responsible land stewardship.
http://www.somagardens.com/nsps/

Richters. Best Canadian herb resource for information and sales.
www.richters.com

Seeds of Diversity Canada. Gardeners who save and share seeds of rare, unusual and heritage plants.
www.seeds.ca/en.htm

Turf Resource Center and The Lawn Institute. The latest data regarding turfgrass.
www.TurfGrassSod.org

The Vine. Carla Allen's weekly gardening column in *The Yarmouth Vanguard*.
www.klis.com/scove/TheVine.htm

Veseys Seed Company. A PEI tradition for over 60 years.
www.veseys.com

New Brunswick Department of Agriculture Soil Laboratory
Experimental Farm
Box 6000, 850 Lincoln Road
Fredericton, NB E3B 5H1
506-453-3495 or 888-662-4742

Nova Scotia Department of Agriculture
Analytical Laboratory Services
Box 550 (mailing only)
2nd floor, 176 College Road
Harlow Institute
Box 550
Truro, NS B2N 5E3
902-893-7444
www.gov.ns.ca/nsaf/qe/labserv/soilsamp.htm

PEI Agricultural Research and Extension Building
Soil and Feed Testing Lab
PO Box 1600, 440 University Avenue
Federal Research Station Bldg.
Charlottetown, PEI C1A 7N3
902-368-5631 or 902-368-5628
www.gov.pe.ca/af/soilfeed/index.asp

New Brunswick:
Fredericton Garden Club
RR#7 Royal Road
Fredericton, NB E3B 4X8
506-459-3206

Fundy Gardeners
Greater Saint John, NB
email: Duncan Kelbaugh
info@brunswicknurseries.com

Granitetown Garden Club
St. George area of Charlotte County, NB
email: Hartley Avery
hartlee@nbnet.nb.ca

Minto Grand Lake Garden Club
506-327-3502
email: Elaine Yeamans
mglgc@yahoo.com

Westmorland Horticultural Society
492 Robinson Street
Moncton, NB E1C 5E6
email: George Griffin
wmhsociety@hotmail.com

Nova Scotia:
Nova Scotia Association of Garden Clubs
61 Harry Drive
Kentville, NS B4N 3V8
902-678-7961

Antigonish Garden Club
c/o Bill and SharonWilgenhof
#407 Old Maryvale Road, RR#3
Antigonish, NS B2G 2L1
902 863-6307
email: willowgarden@gosympatico.ca
www.infinitymedia.ns.ca/willowgarden

St. Margaret's Bay Gardening Club
email: Bay-Club@chebucto.ns.ca
www.chebucto.ns.ca/Recreation/Bay-Gardening/

Prince Edward Island:
Garden Club of Prince Edward Island
PO Box 3203
Charlottetown, PE C1A 7N9
email: peigarden@hotmail.com

Prince Edward Island Rural Beautification Society
Connie Ings
22 Queen's Road
Montague, PE
C0A 2R0
902-838-2683

New Brunswick:
Roosevelt Campobello International Park
Rte. 774, 2.4 km N of Canadian Customs
Fundy Coastal Drive
Campobello Island, NB
506-752-2922
email: info@fdr.net
www.fdr.net

Fredericton Botanic Garden Association
Prospect Street near Hanwell Road
PO Box 57
Fredericton, NB
506-452-9269
email: fbga@nb.aibn.com
www.frederictonbotanicgarden.com

Rockwood Park and Public Gardens
Rockwood Park, main entrance off
Mount Pleasant Avenue
Public Gardens, corner of Seely Street
and Hawthorne Avenue
Saint John, NB
506-658-2883

Kingsbrae Horticultural Garden
220 King Street
St. Andrews, NB
506-529-3335
email: kinghort@nb.aibn.com
www.kingsbraegarden.com

**New Brunswick Botanical Garden, Les
Jardins Park Complex**
7 km N of Edmundston on Rte. 2, Exit 8
15 Principale Street
River Valley Scenic Drive
Saint-Jacques, NB
506-737-5383
email: jardin@umce.ca
http://www.umce.ca/jardin/

**Odell Park, Botanical Garden and
Arboretum**
Fredericton, NB
506-460-2038
www.city.fredericton.nb.ca/community/
parktrail.asp

Nova Scotia:
Historic Gardens
Annapolis Royal
441 St. George Street
Annapolis Royal, NS
902-532-7018
email: admin@historicgardens.com
or hort@historicgardens.com
www.historicgardens.com/index.htm

Blomidon Inn
195 Main Street
Wolfville, NS
902-542-2291
email: innkeepr@blomidon.ns.ca
www.blomidon.ns.ca

Breezy Burros Perennial Gardens
81 Smith Road
Selma, NS
902-261-2190 or 902-261-2499

Halifax Public Gardens
Spring Garden Road and South Park
Street
Halifax, NS
www.destination-ns.com/common/
property.asp?DirectoryID=1957

**River View Herbs, Maitland
Greenhouses**
8907 Hwy 215
Maitland, NS
902-261-2274
www.riverviewherbs.com

Prince Edward Island:
Red Lane Gardens
Off Route 206, West of Iona
RR#3
Belfast, PE
902-659-2478
email: noakes@isn.net
www.redlanegardens.com/rlg_visiting.html

**Ardgowan National Historic Site of
Canada**
Mt. Edward Road at Palmers Lane
Charlottetown, PE
902-566-7626/7050
email: atlantic-parksinfo@pc.gc.ca
www.pc.gc.ca/lhnnhs/pe/ardgowan/
index_e.asp

Kensington Water Gardens
Hwy #2 opposite the Royal Canadian
Legion Home
Kensington, PE
902-836-3336/4356
email: fun@rainbowvalley.pe.ca
www.kata.pe.ca/attract/water/water.htm

Malpeque Gardens
Blue Heron Drive, Route 20
Cabot Beach Provincial Park
Malpeque, PE

Woodleigh Replicas and Gardens
Burlington, RR#2
Kensington, PE
902-836-3401
email: woodleigh@pei.aibn.com
www.woodleighreplicas.com

ACKNOWLEDGEMENTS

We would especially like to thank our fellow garden writers Don Williamson and Laura Peters for their many contributions and discussions.

Thanks to Dick Chiswell, "Mr. Composter," Renforth, NB, Dave Carmichael, the PEI provincial government and Carla Allen, editor of East Coast Gardener, NS, for sharing their advice on seeding dates for various crops. Jim Landry was, as usual, a ready source of hort facts. Thanks also to several members of my garden club, Fundy Gardeners, Judy Whalen, Peter Kinsella, Christine Crowley, and Dick Chiswell, for deepening my pool of knowledge when it proved a bit shallow.

—*Duncan Kelbaugh*

I would like to thank Derek for his continued love and support.

—*Alison Beck*

We are grateful to principal photographers Tamara Eder and Tim Matheson and to the many people who opened their gardens for us to photograph.

We would also like to thank Shane Kennedy, Nancy Foulds, project editor Sandra Bit and book designer/Master Gardener Heather Markham. Thank you to Gerry Dotto for the cover design and to Ian Sheldon for the lovely floral illustrations that grace the corners of every page. Others helped in various ways, close-cropping photos and providing stylistic solutions, and we thank them all.

Cover page photos:
January—spruce bough
February—crabapple branches
March—pasqueflower
April—primroses and tulips
May—crabapple blossoms
June—hosta
July—shrub rose 'The Fairy'
August—dahlias
September—viburnum
October—fall leaves
November—hoarfrost at sunset
December—poinsettias